CARDS.

r doz.

per doz.

by appointment.

rcus, **BUXTON.**

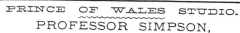

BUXTON
A Pictorial History

BATHING.

AN INVITATION.

COME ye cripples, rich and naked,
  Lame and limping, stiff and sore;
If your bones have ever ached,
  Dip, and they will ache no more;
      Come to Buxton,
      Come to Buxton,
  Here the healing waters pour.

BUXTON
A Pictorial History

Mike Langham
and
Colin Wells

Phillimore

1993

Published by
PHILLIMORE & CO. LTD.
Shopwyke Manor Barn, Chichester, Sussex

ISBN 0 85033 856 5

Printed and bound in Great Britain by
BIDDLES LTD.
Guildford, Surrey

List of Illustrations

Frontispiece: A Victorian letterhead

1. The Crescent, New Baths, 1854
2. Buxton from Corbar before 1854
3. Buxton from Fairfield before 1854
4. Crescent from Irongate, *c.*1840
5. *Royal Hotel, c.*1852
6. Market-place, *c.*1854
7. Higher Buxton, *c.*1854
8. Natural Baths after the rebuild of 1850-54
9. Hot Baths, 1854
10. Hot Baths, *c.*1858
11. Poole's Cavern
12. Market Hall built 1857
13. Hardwick Street, *c.*1860
14. Congregational church, opened in 1861
15. Broadwalk developed from 1861
16. Broadwalk, a later view
17. L.N.W.R. station, opened in 1863
18. L.N.W.R. and Midland stations plan
19. L.N.W.R. station entrance
20. Midland Railway, Monsal Dale viaduct
21. *Leewood Hotel,* opened in 1864
22. Buxton from Corbar, *c.*1862/63
23. Gray's ironmonger's shop, High Street
24. *Palace Hotel* letterheads
25. *Palace Hotel* after enlargement
26. St James's church, built 1870/71
27. St James's church, demolition of the spire, *c.*1896
28. Pavilion Gardens, opened 1871
29. Pavilion Gardens Central Hall, interior
30. Concert Hall, opened 1876
31. Programme for opening of Concert Hall, 1876
32. Concert Hall, exterior
33. Concert Hall, interior
34. Pavilion Gardens skating rink, opened 1876
35. Pavilion Gardens, bandstand and bridge, *c.*1872
36. Pavilion Gardens plan, 1878
37. Devonshire Park Wesleyan chapel, built 1873
38. Devonshire Park, mid-1870s
39. Sparrow Park, *c.*1876
40. Trinity church, built 1873
41. A Buxton winter, *c.*1875
42. Terrace Road, 1870s
43. Market-place, 1870s
44. Market-place, 1870s
45. Terrace Road, *c.*1875
46. London Road tollbar
47. Lower Buxton, 1876
48. Randolph Caldecott in Buxton, 1876
49. Caldecott cartoons: 'The view from St Ann's Cliff' and 'The Promenade'
50. Caldecott cartoon: 'Meet of the Harriers'
51. Caldecott cartoons: 'In the Saloon' and 'A Cardiac Complication'
52. Caldecott cartoons: 'An Incorrigible Beau' and 'March of the men of Buxton'
53. Public water pump
54. *Burlington Hotel,* built 1874
55. *Burlington Hotel* renamed the *Savoy*
56. Burlington Road, commenced in 1876
57. Charity Hot Baths frontage
58. Map showing position of Charity Hot Baths, 1878
59. Map showing internal layout of main baths, 1878
60. Charity Natural Bath
61. Rear entrance Natural Baths, *c.*1872
62. Buxton from Corbar Hill, *c.*1877
63. Lower Buxton map, 1878
64. Turner's memorial, built 1879
65. Turner's memorial demolished
66. Dome construction, Devonshire Hospital, 1880
67. Dome construction, Devonshire Hospital, 1880
68. Devonshire Hospital, architect's plan
69. Devonshire Hospital, external view
70. Dome interior, Devonshire Hospital
71. William, 7th Duke of Devonshire
72. Chatsworth House, Derbyshire
73. George Drewry
74. Letter from George to Frank Drewry
75. Dr. W. H. Robertson
76. Devonshire Hospital, interior
77. Robert Rippon Duke, builder/architect
78. Robert Rippon Duke, collage
79. Josiah Taylor, town clerk
80. Town Hall, opened 1889
81. Town Hall, rear view
82. Edward Chambers Milligan, draper

83. Milligan's drapery shop
84. Post Office, Cavendish Circus, opened 1881
85. Buxton College, built 1881
86. Union Club, built 1886
87. The Hippodrome, opened 1889
88. Pavilion Theatre programme
89. *Peak Hydropathic*, first established in 1880
90. *Peak Hydropathic*, advertisement
91. *Haddon Hall Hydro*, advertisement
92. The *Clarendon Hydropathic*
93. *Malvern House Hydro*
94. *Buxton Hydropathic*, advertisement
95. *Spa Hotel* interior
96. Lumbar douche treatment
97. Buxton douche massage
98. Surge bath
99. Massage bath, Devonshire Hospital
100. Splenic/vapour bath
101. Rain, needle and horizontal jet douche
102. Baxter cartoon: 'At the Natural Baths'
103. Immersion bath, Devonshire Hospital
104. Baxter, the cartoonist
105. Baxter cartoon: 'Promenading inside the Pavilion'
106. Baxter cartoon: 'The Rink'
107. Baxter cartoon of the Concert Hall
108. Baxter cartoon of a bathchairman
109. Baxter cartoon of a drinking well
110. Baxter cartoon: 'The Pump Room at 11 a.m.'
111. Proposed sites for Pump Room
112. Pump Room, built 1893/94
113. Pump Room, interior
114. Pump Room, dispensing pool
115. Pump Room facilities
116. Dressed well, market-place, 1888
117. Well-dressing
118. Well-dressing queen and retinue, 1909
119. Well-dressing queen and her conveyance, 1907
120. Buxton from the Town Hall, 1900
121. Pavilion Gardens
122. Pavilion Gardens, waterfall
123. Victorian children in Pavilion Gardens
124. Serpentine Walks
125. Refreshment kiosk, Pavilion Gardens
126. Solomon's Temple
127. Corbar Wood and walks
128. Sylvan Park
129. Coach trips
130. *Cat and Fiddle Inn*
131. Ice-skating, Pavilion Gardens lake
132. Tennis, Pavilion Gardens
133. Pavilion Gardens curling rink
134. Winter sports at Buxton
135. Hot Baths, 1900
136. Hot Baths and bathchairs, *c.*1905
137. Treatments at Buxton Baths
138. Gentlemen's bath, Natural Baths
139. Gentlemen's corridor, Hot Baths
140. Small plunge bath, Hot Baths
141. Hot Baths exterior, 1909
142. The Tonic Bath
143. Opera House, opened in 1903
144. Opera House programme, 1909
145. King Edward VII and Queen Alexandra visit Buxton
146. The *Empire Hotel*
147. Eagle Parade, 1900
148. Spring Gardens looking east, 1907
149. Spring Gardens looking west, 1907
150. Holme and Ash, Scarsdale Place
151. W. R. Sanders, electrical engineer, advertisement
152. Shufflebotham's ironmonger's, Spring Gardens
153. *Shakespeare Hotel*, exterior
154. *Shakespeare Hotel*, advertisement
155. *Royal Hotel*, advertisement
156. *Crescent Hotel*, assembly room
157. Buxton Central quarry
158. Quarry face, Dowlow, 1908
159. Limekiln, 1908
160. Weathered limestone
161. *Grove Hotel*, *c.*1910
162. Terrace Road
163. Aerial view of Burlington Road
164. Aerial view of Buxton
165. Buxton crest and coat of arms

Foreword

by His Grace the Duke of Devonshire PC MC

I am happy to write a brief foreword to this book which covers the growth of Victorian and Edwardian Buxton, a fascinating period in the history of the town. In the seventy years from 1840, Buxton grew at a remarkable rate and developed into a busy and prosperous inland resort. This growth occurred during the lifetime and with the active support of my ancestors, principally William, the seventh Duke. The history is of great personal interest to me since I have always been actively concerned in the affairs of the town.

The authors, I know, have carried out much research into this period through their study of the architect Robert Rippon Duke who, as part of his professional life, was the architect and surveyor to the Devonshire Buxton Estate for almost forty years. Through this pictorial history the reader may experience the work of our Victorian and Edwardian forefathers, much of which still remains, in laying the foundations of modern Buxton.

Devonshire

Acknowledgements

The authors are grateful for permission to reproduce illustrations from the following individuals and organisations:

The Illustrated London News Picture Library, 1; Mr. Oliver Gomersal, 5, 23, 152; Buxton Museum, Derbyshire County Council, frontispiece, 9, 41, 43, 47, 84, 113, 139, 141, 147; the collection of Derbyshire Library Service, 30, 32-34, 42, 53, 54, 64, 116, 131, 146, 156; J. M. and Chris Bentley, 17, 19 (photos by Harry Townley), 10, 26, 37-39, 44-46, 56, 86, 153; Rod Leach, the Cameraman, 12, 28, 65, 136, 150, 161, 162; Robert Hale Ltd., 13, 129, 157; Valentines of Dundee Limited, 16, 25, 29, 69, 70, 72, 93, 112, 120-23, 126, 128, 130, 148, 149; Devonshire Collection, Chatsworth (reproduced by permission of the Chatsworth Settlement Trustees and permission of the Ordnance Survey), 18, 36, 58, 59, 63, 111; The Duke Papers, Langham & Wells, Buxton, 24, 31, 74, 165; Mr. J. D. Mortin, 27; Rev. Simon Vibert of Trinity church, Buxton, 40; Devonshire Royal Hospital, Buxton, 66-68, 71, 73, 75-77, 79, 82, 97, 99, 103; John Heywood, Manchester, 80 (photo Steward, Buxton), 81, 85 (photos D.C. Latham, Buxton) 135, 155; F. A. Davis & Company, 96, 98, 100, 101; Mrs. Betty Wright, 119; Jarrold & Sons Ltd., 124, 127; University of London Press, 132, 143 (photos J. R. Board, Buxton); The Boots Company plc., 133, 138 (photos Hunter, Buxton); Redland Aggregates Ltd., Dowlow Quarry, 158-60; by kind permission of the High Peak Borough Council, 115, 134, 137; the Documentary Photographic Archive, Manchester, 35, 61. All other illustrations are from the authors' collection. Much care has been taken to obtain permissions to use illustrations and the authors apologise in advance for the accidental omission of any acknowledgement.

The authors would like to thank Mr. Oliver Gomersal for his very helpful critique of the manuscript and the encouragement which he and his wife Marjorie have given us during Saturday afternoon teas and tutorials when we have met to discuss our research; long may they continue! We offer our thanks to many friends and associates who have helped with the preparation of this book, in particular, Mick and Chris Bentley who have been most generous in providing early original photographs, Tom Askey and Peter Day of the Devonshire Collections, and the staff of the Local Studies Library and Museum at Buxton.

Introduction

Buxton, in the High Peak of Derbyshire, sits in a bowl at about one thousand feet above sea level surrounded by mountains and is itself a mountain spa. The natural mineral water of Buxton emerges from a group of springs at a constant temperature of 82 degrees Fahrenheit and is, thus, a thermal water. There are also cold springs and a supply of chalybeate (iron bearing) water.

Whilst the history of this inland resort can be traced as far back as the Mesolithic (middle stone age) period of early man, one of the most significant periods in the development of the town was the 70 years from 1840 to 1910 – the Victorian/Edwardian age of industry and innovation. This book is about that period and is an attempt to capture, in words and contemporary illustrations, the phenomenal growth of Buxton itself. The three villages of Fairfield, Burbage and Harpur Hill, which today form an integral part of the town, are not explicitly included in this history.

The story of Victorian Buxton should be set in the context of its earlier history if we are to have some feel for the growth of settlement, village and town to see how and why Buxton should have become such an important Victorian spa.

The evidence of Mesolithic man suggests a settlement dating to about 5000 B.C. and archaeological finds in the Peak District around the settlement show habitation through the Neolithic, Bronze and Iron Ages to the time of the Romans. Buxton in Roman times was known as Aquae Arnemetiae, which translates as the 'waters of the Goddess of the Grove', and the term 'aquae' is used by the Romans for one other town only, that of Bath which was called Aquae Sulis. From the historical evidence we can say that Buxton was a civilian settlement of some importance, situated on the intersection of several roads and providing bathing facilities in warm mineral waters. In short, it was a Roman spa. An important find of coins near the probable site of the Roman bath, in 1975, indicates that the Romans inhabited Buxton for most of the time they occupied Britain.

Place-names in and around Buxton, and Anglo-Saxon finds in burial mound excavations, suggest a continuing inhabitation of the area and probable use of the warm mineral waters. Buxton is not mentioned in Domesday Book though, at the time, it was primarily a cattle pasturing place and may not have been of sufficient interest, in revenue terms, to King William's commissioners. The name Buxton can be dated to about 1100 when Bucstones or Buckestones is first recorded on a foundation charter for land given by William Peverel to found Lenton Abbey in Nottinghamshire. Later medieval records show the existence of a holy well at Buxton and the valuation taken for King Henry VIII in 1536 showed the well to be worth 40 marks (about £26), a not inconsiderable sum. The well and chapel did not escape the attentions of Thomas Cromwell, the Chief Minister to King Henry, and on his orders it was plundered and closed down by Sir William Bassett of Langley in 1538.

The well was not closed for long, however, and in the Elizabethan era Buxton enjoyed considerable fame as a spa. Mary Queen of Scots visited to take the waters on several occasions during the time she was a prisoner in England. Her custodian, the Earl of Shrewsbury, who was married to Bess of Hardwick, built the hall over the bath in Buxton to provide accommodation. It is likely that Buxton was a centre of some intrigue at this time; plots were hatched in support of the Scottish queen and there were many notable visitors from the Elizabethan court including Lord Burghley, the Earl of Sussex, and the Earl of Leicester, a favourite of Queen Elizabeth. In 1572 Dr. John Jones wrote the first medical book on Buxton waters entitled *The Benefit of the Auncient Bathes of Buckstones*. From that time many others wrote on the curative value of the warm waters and from these accounts it can be seen how Buxton continued to develop as a spa through the 17th century.

The 18th century was to see an upsurge of interest in bathing and water treatment with both inland and coastal towns becoming fashionable resorts. Buxton did not rival Bath in these terms, however, until the 5th Duke of Devonshire decided to provide greatly enhanced facilities in the shape of the Crescent, which offered hotels, lodging houses and an assembly room. This magnificent building was designed by the York architect, John Carr, and built between 1780 and 1784. The Great Stables, now the Devonshire Royal Hospital, were completed in 1789. By 1820, with a population of under one thousand, Buxton could still be described as a village and facilities were still modest. Hall Bank, built largely in the 1790s, provided lodging houses and the Square, built 1806, offered more substantial town houses. In addition to the *Hall* and those in the Crescent, there were other hotels including the *Grove* and the *George*, the *Eagle* and the *Shakespeare*, together with a number of inns and ordinary lodging houses. The baths offered quite limited facilities, three gentlemen's, two ladies' and a charity bath, though there were also hot baths, built in about 1818 and, on the Macclesfield road, a cold plunging or tonic bath.

Victorian Buxton

In 1840 Dr. A. B. Granville, a writer on spas, described Buxton as having a shortage of good, comfortable lodging houses and he made a number of suggestions for improvement which, to some extent, anticipated the development of the spa from this time onwards. From 1850 Buxton began to grow from a village to a busy and fashionable spa, an inland resort whose visitors increased the population threefold during the season. Many people came to take the wide range of treatments on offer at the natural and thermal baths or at one of the several hydropathic hotels. Others came to rest and recuperate, yet others to enjoy the sport and pastimes available in the Derbyshire Peak District. The shaping of the town was greatly influenced by a small number of notable characters including the Dukes of Devonshire, principally the 6th ('the Bachelor Duke') and the 7th, their Agents, and Dr. W. H. Robertson, author of the extremely popular *Handbook to the Peak of Derbyshire* and longtime Chairman of the Devonshire Hospital Charity. Other notables were members of the Local Board, Directors of the Buxton Improvements Company, Trustees of the Devonshire Hospital and local businessmen. A number of them are featured in this pictorial history and the story of one, a certain Robert Rippon Duke, runs as a continuing thread throughout. R. R. Duke was born in Hull and came to Buxton in 1849. In the following 50 years he not only developed himself professionally through site agent, builder, surveyor to full blown architect, but also exerted a very significant influence on the architecture and the social fabric of Victorian Buxton – an influence which has not, until now, been fully recognised.

The *Royal Hotel*

Situated on the corner of Spring Gardens, the *Royal* is probably the earliest Victorian building of note and was built between 1849 and 1852 on the site of the former *Angel Inn*. It was designed by Samuel Worth, a builder/architect from Sheffield, for Andrew Brittlebank, a solicitor and businessman of Winster in Derbyshire. Brittlebank's agent and adviser in the venture was another Derbyshire businessman, William Wyatt, a lead mine owner, mineral agent and solicitor of Foolow and, on the recommendation of the architect, they employed R. R. Duke to act as building supervisor. The *Royal Hotel* was a significant architectural achievement in its time, built to complement the curve of the Crescent and, although now occupied by shops and offices, much of the original fabric remains. In 1851 Buxton could be described as having an old town, formed around the market-place, and a new town constituted by the more fashionable developments around the Crescent and the Baths in lower Buxton. Adam, in his *Gem of the Peak*, gives a good description of the shops and superior accommodation situated in and around the Crescent. He refers to '... the new *Royal Hotel*, a splendid building, lately erected ...' and lists the *Shakespeare* in Spring Gardens, *St Anne's* and the *Crescent* hotels, the *Hall*, the *George* and, in Irongate, the *Grove*. Little description is given of Higher Buxton: the *Eagle* and *Kings Head* in the market-place are described as good class hotels and, under taverns and public houses, there are listed the *Cheshire Cheese*, the *Sun* and the *Queens Head*, with other good and comfortable houses not named. The population of the town (excluding the adjacent village of Fairfield) was about 1,600 and it is likely that more than that number of visitors could be accommodated in the season; thus we find that virtually every house is listed as a lodging house in the directories. The 6th Duke of Devonshire, 'the Bachelor Duke', invested extensively in Buxton and continued the work of his predecessors, but left the detail to his Agents, Phillip Heacock and Sidney Smithers. Heacock died in 1851 and his impressive monument in St John's churchyard was erected under the supervision of R. R. Duke.

New Natural and Hot Baths

Between 1852 and 1854 the Baths underwent a major re-design and re-build under the architect to the Devonshire Estate, Henry Currey. Two different styles of architecture were selected: the natural wing was built of stone from the neighbourhood and the single façade had no windows or doors, though three fountains were set in fluted niches to give life to the elevation. The hot baths wing was built of iron and glass with an impressive colonnade to the front. Inside, the baths were well finished and equipped; the Natural Baths provided separate public and private baths for ladies and gentlemen and separate charity baths for patients of the Devonshire Hospital. The largest Gentlemen's Public Bath was fed with natural mineral water through perforations in the marble bottom and it was considered important to use the natural gases in the water as part of the treatment. The Hot Baths provided public and private accommodation for each sex and for charity patients also a cold swimming bath. The usual medical facilities of the time were provided in both the baths buildings, including douche, shower and vapour treatments, and appropriate dressing rooms. This major extension to the baths complex allowed Buxton to offer very up-to-date facilities necessary for the development of the spa. Over the next 60 years several modifications and improvements were made to the baths facilities in order to increase the accommodation for those seeking treatment.

Growing Facilities

During the 1850s a number of other facilities were developed. A design for the development of the Park with fashionable housing was reputedly produced by Joseph Paxton, though it was not substantially developed until much later in the century. The building of the Quadrant began in about 1853 and, although subsequent building spanned six or seven years, the same architectural style was maintained, as can be seen today. Another early development was Hardwick Street which was begun in 1858.

A public pump was erected opposite the Crescent in 1852. This was a double pump supplying natural tepid water one side and cold the other. In 1857 Higher Buxton benefited from the building of the Market Hall on the site of the present Town Hall. Designed by Henry Currey, the Market Hall was built by R. R. Duke in partnership with Samuel Turner. It burned down in September 1885. Other growth in Higher Buxton included the building of lodging houses on Bath Street in the early 1860s to cater for seasonal visitors.

In 1855 the Buxton, Fairfield and Burbage Mechanics Institute was formed with Robert Rippon Duke as its first president. This was intended to provide instruction for adults and youths of all classes, especially those engaged in trade and manual labour. A library and reading room were provided together with lectures on various subjects and the Institute provided a valuable public education for about twelve years. Banking facilities in the town had been limited until 1856 when a branch of the Sheffield and Rotherham Joint Stock Banking Company was established in Spring Gardens. In 1857 the Buxton Savings Bank was established for the safe custody and increase of small savings of the 'industrious classes'.

In 1859 Buxton established its Local Board of Health – an early form of the Local Authority permitted by an Act of Parliament of 1858. Josiah Taylor was the first, and very long-serving Clerk to the Local Board, U.D.C. and Borough Council, receiving the freedom of the new Borough in 1918.

Travel was mainly by coach or cart via the network of turnpikes which served the town. In 1856 the *King's Head* coach office offered services on the *Royal Peveril* and *Celerity* to Manchester. Mr. James Brown of the *Cheshire Cheese* inn offered daily services to and from Manchester on the *Express* and *Wonder* coaches. Other services connected the town with Crewe, Macclesfield and Rowsley, the latter having a station on the Midland Railway line to Derby.

The Cromford and High Peak Railway Company offered cheap travel between Wirksworth and Buxton by adding a passenger carriage to their goods trains. An omnibus provided a connection between the arriving coaches in Buxton and the C.H.P.R. station at Ladmanlow, one and a half miles out of the town.

Advent of the Railways

In the early 1860s provision for the spiritual needs of townsfolk and visitors were extended in the building of the Catholic church of St Anne on Terrace Road and the Congregational church on Hardwick Terrace. The former was designed by J. J. Scholes, though the architect Henry Currey may have been involved in its design. Currey was the architect of the Congregational church. Both of these churches were built by the building firm of R. R. Duke. The addition of Turkish baths in the hot bath department of the Crescent in 1862 offered further medical facilities, though it would appear that these were short-lived, as by 1866 they had made way for shops in the Devonshire Colonnade.

The town was bustling at this time and poised to increase its trade and prosperity with the coming of the railways in 1863. A survey of Buxton trades in 1862 shows that the town had two banks, a bazaar, a brazier, a builder, a china and earthenware dealer, a coal agent, an ironmonger, two newspapers (the *Herald* and the *Advertiser*), a photographer, a general printer, two railway booking offices (though there was, as yet, no railway), a refreshment room, four shampooers (masseurs), a solicitor, a tobacconist and two wine and spirit merchants. These trades were in addition to the more usual bakers, butchers and so on, and there were also several petrifaction works making and selling ornaments made from fluorspar, Ashford marble, Blue John and other local stones. The bazaar was Anzani's toy shop, the builder was Robert Rippon Duke and the solicitor would have been J. W. Taylor of 1 Hardwick Terrace, who was founder trustee of Trinity church and a trustee of the Devonshire Hospital and Buxton Bath Charity.

The photographer was Barrowclough W. Bentley, a pioneer in the profession who operated, principally, from the Quadrant but had a branch in St Ann's Square, Manchester. B. W. Bentley was the most outstanding of the Victorian Buxton photographers and became nationally known for his artistic collections of the Peak District and Chatsworth House. Whilst little of his early work survives, we are fortunate in being able to feature some of his photographs in this book.

Continuing the description of the town, there were shopping areas in the Crescent, where Bright's well-known jeweller's shop was situated, the Hot Bath Colonnade, Quadrant, Terrace Road and Hardwick Street. The main shopping areas in Higher Buxton were Eagle Parade, Concert Place, Scarsdale Place, High Street and Dunmore Square which housed a mixed collection of shops on the market-place opposite the Market Hall.

Of the utilities, the Buxton Gas Coke and Coal Company, originally established in 1851, was re-constituted as a limited company in 1862. The reservoirs were owned by the Devonshire estate and during 1860 a sewerage system was designed by Robert Rawlinson who was active in public works in Lancashire in the 1860s and awarded Knight Commander of the Bath some years later – an appropriate award one might think!

The most significant occurrence in the early 1860s, however, was the arrival of the railways in 1863. The Midland Railway Company engineered a line from Matlock to Buxton which was opened on 30 May, whilst the Stockport, Disley and Whaley Bridge Railway Company (chiefly owned by L.N.W.R.) opened its line from Whaley Bridge to Buxton on the same day. Both companies held luncheons to celebrate the event and it would seem that Sir Joseph Paxton attended both. The stations at Buxton were similar in external design though getting the two great railway companies to agree was not without difficulty and took the persuasive power of Paxton, who intervened in the negotiations to secure a compromise. The fan-windowed façade of the L.N.W.R. station which remains today may be said to show Paxton's influence.

Undoubtedly the arrival of the railways provided the much needed communication link between Buxton and its potential spa treatment and tourist clientele; the town began to develop rapidly to meet the tourist trade. A new hotel, the *Leewood*, was opened in 1864 by Mr. Brian Bates who also ran the *Old Hall* and *Royal* hotels. The *Railway Hotel* in Bridge Street was opened in the same year and considerable extensions were made to the *Seven Stars Inn* in Higher Buxton to accommodate the increasing numbers, who 'as excursionists flock to Buxton'. The owner of the *Buxton Advertiser*, John Cumming Bates, extended his business by the building of a new printing office, designed by R. R. Duke, in Eagle Street, just off the market-place.

Further improvements were made to the Hot and Natural Baths (mainly to the glass roofs) and the Tonic Bath, a cold bath situated at the bottom of Bath Road, was offering treatments, though it had a chequered commercial career.

The *Palace Hotel*

The most important residential provision of this time, and still a major landmark, was the *Palace Hotel*. This was originally known as the *Buxton Hotel* and was built in its own grounds adjacent to the two railway stations. It was designed by Henry Currey and built as a speculative venture between 1863 and 1867. The original company got into financial difficulties (probably not helped by the fact that the country as a whole went through a very severe financial crisis in 1866 with a major loss of confidence in speculative ventures) and the hotel was sold by auction in November 1867. The new company renamed the hotel the *Palace* and the shareholders included the Duke of Devonshire and two of the L.N.W.R. directors as well as prominent local businessmen. The Company Secretary was R. R. Duke who had also been Clerk of Works during the building. The *Palace Hotel* proved to be a prosperous business and was subsequently extended and improved to include the addition of a north wing and a new dining room, both of which were designed by R. R. Duke.

The Broadwalk

An important addition was the Broadwalk which was extensively developed between 1861 and the early 1870s to become one of the most fashionable Victorian terraces in the town, in an unrivalled position overlooking the pleasure gardens and pavilion. In 1861 the present Broadwalk was laid out as the new Cavendish Terrace, with the first three houses, known as Cavendish Villas, erected for Mr. Barnard, a wine and spirit merchant and sometime member of the Local Board. By 1864 there were 10 dwellings, including Milton House, given as no. 9, and nos. 4, 5 and 6 were in the process of erection; all the properties were listed as private lodging houses. The directory in Dr. Robertson's *Buxton Guide of 1866* lists nos. 1 to 11 which include Milton, Cavendish and Derby houses together with nos. 14 and 15, known as Lake Villas which, by 1868, had become 15 and 16 to make way for Stanley Terrace occupying nos. 12 to 14. Also newly built were Dalton House and Cambridge Villas.

It is interesting to look at the style of the many houses remaining on the Broadwalk from this period including Grosvenor Terrace, Cavendish and Derby Houses, Stanley Terrace or Villas (now the *Sandringham Hotel*), Lake Villas (now simply nos. 16 and 17), Dalton House (now the *Hartington Hotel*) and Cambridge Villas (now known as Roseleigh and Sherwood).

Buxton Enters the 1870s

A measure of the growth of Buxton may be had from comparing the population statistics. These show that between 1851 and 1861 the population increased by 50 per cent and in the following 10 years to 1871 by a further 35 per cent. This may be set against the growth for Derbyshire as a whole of 15 and 12 per cent for the same periods. The physical growth of the town up to 1870 is very neatly summed up in a leader article in the *Buxton Advertiser* for Saturday 23 April 1870:

> ... On all sides the town has grown and spread. In Spring Gardens we find new houses and shops, the enlarged Shakespeare Hotel, the Royal Hotel and Winster Place, the new street (Bridge Street) with its Railway Hotel and Sylvan Park. Then there are the handsome houses on Hardwick Street and Hardwick Terrace with the pretty Congregational Church; nearly the whole of Terrace Road has also been erected with Belmont Terrace, St Ann's Square and the Market House; the houses on Hall Bank are double the number they were in '52 and what was the top then is pushed into the middle. Then there are the Quadrant, the Bank, the railway stations, the Palace Hotel and the Devonshire Hospital and grounds, the Leewood Hotel and grounds and the handsome houses and numerous villas in Devonshire Park or dotted on the sides of the southward sloping Corbar Hill, together with the handsome and commodious erections in St John's Road; the renovated George Hotel; the additions and improvements at the Old Hall and St Anne's Hotels and the whole of the Broad Walk houses; Hartington street with its Malvern Hydropathic establishment; Fountain Street, Torr Street, West Parade etc. to testify to rapid growth. Nor has Higher Buxton been behind the rest of the town, the spirit and enterprise of some of its residents have improved and developed it in a manner highly creditable to them as shown by the number of handsome houses and excellent shops. The garden of the Eagle Hotel occupies a large space, of Eagle 'Gravel' (A name now lost in that of 'Parade') and other improvements also show that Higher Buxton will hold its own with the rest of the town. There are the comfortable looking houses in London Road, an improved West Street, a new Bath Street (soon to be graced with a new church St James's) ...

More Churches

St James's church was built in Bath Road in 1870-71 in answer to the shortage of Anglican facilities. It was designed by M. H. Taylor to seat 800 and was a fine looking church with a lofty interior. By about 1896 the spire had become unsafe and was taken down and the church was fully demolished in the early 1960s; the site is now occupied by a health clinic.

In 1872 R. R. Duke was asked to prepare plans for a small chapel on Hardwick Mount by the solicitor, Mr. J. W. Taylor. For a number of reasons, including the building of St James's church, it was decided to build a Chapel of Ease for those of the town and visitors who wanted an Evangelical and quiet form of public worship. The chapel, designed by R. R. Duke, forms the southern portion of the present building, the nave, and was built in 1873 by Messrs. Hinch and Bennett at a cost of £614. Trinity church was subsequently extended with a new transept in 1883 and by the addition of a tower in 1906.

The Devonshire Park Wesleyan chapel, situated on the corner of Devonshire and Marlborough roads, was completed in 1873. The architects were Mellor and Sutton of Stockport. This chapel was described as a large and noble building in the Gothic style with a tower and an octagonal spire. Inside there was a rear gallery above a nave which led to an apsidal chancel. This chapel was demolished in about 1968 and the site used for housing.

Devonshire Park

From the early 1870s the Duke of Devonshire's estate was selling land in Buxton for building, a practice which was to continue through the rest of the 19th century. One of the earlier examples was the Devonshire Park which was extensively developed for fashionable residential housing. In fact the Devonshire Park, on the east side of the Manchester Road, was developed earlier than the Park itself. By 1878 there was a number of substantial residences, many of which can be seen today. In Marlborough Road at least four houses date to this time; they are: The Laurels, Balmoral, Spring Bank and Fairleigh. The present nursing home on Devonshire Road, was originally built as two villas called Hamilton and Arnside and at the top of the road is Flintsbank, now called Hollinsbank and Southbank. Bordering Devonshire Park on Manchester Road are Thornbank, Park House (home of R. R. Duke) and Beaufort Villas.

Other building of note in the 1870s included the development of Bridge Street in 1870 with cottage properties, the formation of St James's Terrace and the building of the *Burlington Hotel* at the lower end of Hall Bank in 1874. The present Burlington Road was laid out in 1876 but completed only from St John's Road to halfway down. The road was not fully completed until the 1890s and the two houses built in 1876, Rockavon and Buckingham (now forming the *Buckingham Hotel*), remained the only development on Burlington Road for some years.

Other high-class housing was provided on St John's Road whilst working-class and artisan accommodation was erected in Dale Terrace, Dale Street and Bennet Street which was developed by a local doctor, Robert Ottiwell Gifford Bennet.

Turner's Memorial

A notable landmark in the town, seen on many Victorian prints but now sadly gone, was the memorial to Samuel Turner which stood in the centre of the road opposite the entrance to the Hot Baths. Samuel Turner was an important figure in the town: he was a sub-agent to the Devonshire Buxton Estate for some years, Trustee and Treasurer of the Devonshire Hospital, member of the Local Board, Director of the Buxton Improvements Company and, for more than thirty years, a churchwarden at St John's church. When he died in 1876 his longtime friend R. R. Duke raised a subscription and designed a stone and marble drinking fountain with suitable description of the townsman's worth. It was unveiled in 1879 by the town's best known authority on Buxton water, Dr. W. H. Robertson. Unfortunately, this monument was irreparably damaged by a van in 1959 and did not last, perhaps, quite as long as Samuel Turner's friends had intended!

The Pavilion Gardens

Buxton had, for many years, a town band to entertain the visitors, which was paid for by the Duke of Devonshire as one of a number of commitments made to the town. The 7th Duke was, however, anxious to see the town more self-sufficient and his endeavours in this respect resulted in the formation of the Buxton Improvements Company. He donated 12 acres of land free of charge and offered half the cost of building a winter garden. The Improvements Company was formed in 1870 and developed the land into gardens and walks and erected a glass and iron pavilion in which to hold concerts and for promenading in wet weather. The building was designed by Edward Milner and his son Henry. Milner senior had trained under Crystal Palace architect, Joseph Paxton, whose influence can be seen. The Winter Garden and grounds were opened to the public in May 1871 and became an instant success, so much so that as early as 1872 there were complaints of overcrowding. In that year the company approached R. R. Duke to design an extension. He submitted plans for a large octagonal concert hall in a similar style to the rest of the building and for a roller skating rink in the grounds. The Concert Hall and rink were built during 1875-76 and opened in August 1876 by His Grace the Duke of Devonshire in a suitably lavish ceremony befitting the importance of the investment. The Pavilion Gardens became a great attraction in the tradition of Victorian public parks and walks; they were, and still are, a great asset to the town. The roller skating gave way to changing fashions over the years and the rink was also used for ice-skating and curling.

New Charity Baths

The development of Buxton as an inland resort centred chiefly on the natural mineral waters and the range of treatments available including douches, hot air or turkish baths, moor and peat baths and various massage and localised applications. The Natural and Hot Baths in the Crescent were owned by the Devonshire Estate and offered a considerable return to the Duke of Devonshire. These baths contained separate facilities for charity patients at the Devonshire Hospital who could take the water treatment under the Buxton Bath Charity by being referred to the hospital by a charity subscriber. During the early 1870s the baths became more and more crowded until a point was reached where the Duke's Buxton Agent began to explore the possibility of using the room taken up by the ladies' and men's charity baths by moving such patients elsewhere. The original suggestion was to build some new baths at the Devonshire Hospital and find ways of pumping the natural mineral water from its source up to the hospital grounds. The Chairman of the Devonshire Hospital and Buxton Bath Charity, Dr. W. H. Robertson, was insistent, however, that transporting the water so far would have the effect of seriously lessening its medicinal properties. There followed a protracted negotiation phase during which the Duke of Devonshire became increasingly impatient with the good doctor. In the end, in true Victorian style, a compromise was reached and this resulted in the provision of new Charity Hot Baths in George Street and a Natural Charity Bath built under the road at the back of the *Old Hall Hotel* but close to the water source. The Hot Baths were fed with the overflow from the main baths in the Crescent and times were arranged when the water could be taken. The new baths were designed by R. R. Duke. Thus the Duke could extend his facilities for paying patients whilst still providing for charity patients and, although the Hot Baths provision was quite reasonable, the Natural Bath facilities must have been very cramped in comparison with the original arrangements.

The overcrowding in the pump rooms led to the provision of a drinking well for charity patients, also in George Street, which was designed by R. R. Duke and built in

1881 as part of the major extensions to the Devonshire Hospital. The buildings which housed the Charity Drinking Well and the Hot Baths can be seen today, as can the remains of the Charity Natural Bath, but now this is mostly boarded up.

Working and Learning in Victorian Buxton

The Hardwick Square Infant and Junior Board schools were opened in 1875, sometime before the area was developed with fashionable housing. There was also a number of private schools including the Holm Leigh School for Boys in Devonshire Park and the Buxton Classical School in the Broadwalk. These also took the children of visitors to the town. Plans were laid in 1879 for a grammar school with master's house which was the development of the present site of Buxton College. The college, originally on the market-place, moved from premises on the corner of Market Street and South Street in 1881 to its present position on College Road.

The 'spa' industry, both medical and tourist, provided both direct and indirect employment for many of the inhabitants; in addition to hotels and other accommodation, there was a surprising number of livery stables, also laundries, bathchair proprietors and many similar services. The next biggest source of employment was quarrying, an industry which virtually encircled the town. This was mainly limestone, but there was also coal mining just outside the town. The railways provided the conditions for expansion and many quarries were developed from the mid-1860s. By 1891 there were at least 17 limestone quarries around Buxton and the fierce competition caused many of the quarry owners to agree to work together to form the Buxton Lime Firms Ltd. which opened offices in the Quadrant. Limestone was used for a wide variety of purposes, one of the more curious of which was to weather stones into odd shapes for use in rockeries, and many such stones can still be seen in the gardens of Victorian Buxton houses.

Through the 1880s there was much development in Higher Buxton including middle-class housing between Hardwick Street and South Street, the growth of Hardwick Square, the expansion of Market Street, houses and shops in High Street and the extension of West Street. In this expansion of the town, building work must have provided a significant additional source of employment.

The Devonshire Hospital Extensions

In 1857 the Devonshire Hospital was established with the donation, by the 6th Duke of Devonshire (1790-1858), of part of the Great Stables to the trustees of the Bath Charity. The hospital occupied the first floor with the ground floor remaining as stables, a less than hygienic arrangement not helped by the fact that the only access to the first floor was by stairs. The trustees began what was to be the long process of persuading the 7th Duke to relinquish the rest of the building so that it might all be turned into a hospital. They finally succeeded in 1877 and applied to the Cotton Districts Convalescent Fund, a charity which had its origins in the cotton famine relief in Lancashire during the American Civil War. The hospital trustees secured a grant of £5,000 but this proved to be far short of the early estimate of £10,650 drawn up by R. R. Duke for the conversion. There followed a series of negotiations to secure greater funds from the charity in return for the provision of more charity beds for the treatment of Lancashire mill workers and others. Ultimately a grant of £24,000 was obtained and the work went ahead between 1879 and 1881. R. R. Duke's design included the removal of two internal walls and the construction of a concrete gallery to enlarge considerably the ward space, the whole building to be enclosed by a circular domed roof. There was strong opposition from some of the governors of the Cotton Districts Convalescent Fund to the idea of the domed roof, mainly on the grounds of cost, but the design was eventually carried through and became an architectural 'tour de force'. The area covered by the dome is just half an acre and, at 164 ft. in diameter, it is larger than the Pantheon, Rome (142 ft.), St Peter's, Rome (139 ft.) and St Paul's, London (112 ft.). At the time of building it was the largest unsupported dome in the world. The conversion included a clock tower erected as a testimonial to Dr. W. H. Robertson, longtime Chairman and Medical Adviser of the Hospital Charity. The completion of the hospital extensions was not without some difficulty for the architect. The experience of the Tay Bridge railway disaster caused him to undertake re-drilling of the ironwork and the contract proved very difficult to control in respect of builder's extras, bringing the cost of the conversion to about £27,000 and resulting in a protracted arbitration case. Nevertheless, this hospital stands today as a monument to the great courage and skill of the Victorian architect and, when completed, it was considered a great asset by the trustees. Further additions followed, including an accident ward in 1900, and in 1905 King Edward VII and Queen Alexandra toured the hospital on their visit to Buxton.

The Hydropathic Treatments

The reliance of water treatments upon the unique mineral and/or thermal properties was challenged in the 1830s by the German practitioner Vincenz Priessnitz who developed treatments using cold water combined with dietary regimes. This gave rise to the hydropathic movement and paved the way for hydros which offered a wide range of treatments using ordinary water, including Turkish, Russian, electrical, vapour, douche and sitz baths. By the 1880s Buxton had a number of hydros, though they had a relatively short and very competitive commercial life, declining in popularity by the late 1920s. The largest was the *Buxton Hydropathic* in Hartington Road which had 260 rooms and extensive facilities. Others included the *Royal* in Spring Gardens, the *Haddon Hall* and *Olivers* on London Road, the *Corbar Hill* or *Clarendon* on Manchester Road (now part of the Devonshire Hospital) and the *Peak Hydro* on Terrace Road, now the Peak buildings and British Legion club.

Healthy Pastimes

The increasing popularity of Buxton called for further facilities to be provided in water treatment and leisure. In 1884 the Improvements Company held an open lawn tennis tournament which continued as an annual event for many years and hosted the All-England Ladies' Doubles Championship until 1953. In 1885 the first county cricket match was held with Derbyshire playing Cheshire and the High Peak Golf Club was founded in 1886. In that year the Union Club in Water Street, designed by the architect W. R. Bryden, was opened as a non-political gentlemen's club for use by residents and visitors. W. R. Bryden also designed the Playhouse (originally called the Entertainment Stage) which opened in 1889.

An unusual pastime in Buxton was that of curling, which took place on the frozen roller skating rink in the Pavilion Gardens. In 1895 the Buxton Curling Club was founded by Dr. Graeme Dickson of Wye House Asylum. In the winter months tobogganing, skiing and ice-skating were very popular. Less energetic pastimes included walking and driving in the surrounding Peak countryside. A number of charabanc and coach services operated to places such as the Goyt Valley, Ravensdale, Millers Dale, the *Cat and Fiddle Inn* and Lovers Leap in Ashwood Dale.

An ancient Derbyshire custom, its origins lost in time, is that of well-dressing. The wells and springs in Derbyshire villages are decorated, during an annual festival, to give thanks for the supply of pure water. In Buxton, well-dressing began in about 1840 and continued throughout the Victorian and Edwardian periods. Festivities included the dressing of the three wells with pictures made up of flowers and leaves, the selection and crowning of the well-dressing queen and the arrival of the funfair. The town would be festooned with bunting put up by tradesmen, and people would dress up to join the procession around the town. The custom still continues today and takes place during July.

The New Pump Room

The two well or pump rooms, providing thermal and chalybeate water for drinking, were situated in the Crescent adjacent to the Natural Baths. These became progressively overcrowded and plans were laid for the completion of a new pump room to be situated opposite the Crescent at the bottom of the slopes. The new pump room, opened in June 1894 by the 8th Duke of Devonshire, was the last great gift to the town from the 7th Duke who died before it was completed. Buxton now had extensive medical bathing facilities, mineral drinking water and a range of hydrotherapeutic treatments. Visitors flocked to the inland spa; the *Buxton Advertiser* for 4 August 1894 lists the names of visitors at four hydros and no less than 16 hotels. Small wonder that the local authority felt it necessary to have a substantial Town Hall. This was designed by William Pollard and built by the local builder, James Salt, on the site of the old Market Hall. It was opened in 1889 and stands today a typical statement of late Victorian achievement and industry.

The 20th Century

By 1900 electricity had come to the town and was installed in the Pavilion Gardens and Concert Hall. An impressive new tea and refreshment room was also located in the gardens. The National Telephone Company provided a service for a number of the hotels and businesses. Contemporary advertisements give telephone numbers consisting of a single digit – a far cry from the long numbers of today!

The Hot Baths were re-modelled in 1900, the glass and iron exterior being replaced by a classical stone frontage. In 1904 the 8th Duke of Devonshire sold the Hot and Natural Baths to the Council for a yearly rent of £2,431, to be paid for 60 years. In 1909 the glass colonnading was replaced on the Hot Baths.

A most substantial new development at the turn of the century was the *Empire Hotel*, built in the Park by Spiers and Pond at a reputed cost of £130,000. The company was well known for its chain of refreshment rooms on the railways. The *Empire* was very luxurious and opened during the season only from 1903. It had a short commercial life and became a discharge depot for Canadian troops after the First World War. It was demolished, after falling into disrepair, in 1964.

In 1901 the Gardens Company gave approval for the expenditure of £25,000 on a new theatre and entrance to the Pavilion Gardens. This was to be the Opera House, described as 'a real gem of a theatre' and designed by Frank Matcham (1854-1920), a prolific theatre designer in his day. This beautiful theatre was opened in 1903, the first play being *Mrs Willoughby's Kiss*, a domestic drama in four acts by Mr. Frank Stayton. The Opera House underwent major restoration in 1979, and in the same year began the annual International Opera Festival which continues as a major festival of the arts in Buxton today.

The official guide book of 1909 shows the buoyancy of the town at that time. The pump room had five massive silvered fountains; chalybeate water was available for drinking or bathing and the extensive range of treatments on offer in the Hot and Natural Baths included many imported from Austrian and German spas. A wide variety of hotels and lodgings were available from the modest to the very exclusive and there was provision for entertainment in the theatres and Pavilion Gardens, and for sport in both winter and summer. In addition to all this, visitors could enjoy the majestic and varied countryside of the Peak District in drives and walks.

This pictorial history is set out broadly in a chronological order. Mainly contemporary illustrations have been used to suit the subject being described but, inevitably, on some occasions we have had to use later material. Nevertheless, the overall aim is to present a picture of the continuing development of Buxton during the Victorian/Edwardian period.

Some Further Reading on Buxton's History

Adam, William, *Gem of the Peak* (1851) Moorland Publishing Company, Derbyshire, 1973.

Bishop, M. J., *Buxton in Old Picture Postcards*, European Library, Netherlands, 1984.

Goodacre, J. A., *Buxton Old and New*, privately published, 1928.

Granville, A. B., *Spas of England: 2 The Midlands and South* (1841), Adams & Dart, Bath, 1971 edition.

Grundy Heape, R., *Buxton under the Dukes of Devonshire*, Robert Hale, London, 1948.

Langham, M. J., and Wells, C., *Buxton Waters – A History of Buxton the Spa*, J. H. Hall & Sons Ltd., Derby, 1986.

Leach, J., *The Book of Buxton*, Barracuda Books, Buckingham, 1987.

McCoola, Ros, *Theatre in the Hills*, Caron Publications, Chapel-en-le-Frith, Derbys., 1984.

Pevsner, N., *The Buildings of England – Derbyshire*, Penguin Books, Harmondsworth, Middx., 1986.

Robertson, W. H., *A handbook to the Peak of Derbyshire*, J. C. Bates, Buxton, 1854 and subsequent editions.

1. This is probably the most popular view of Buxton. The Crescent, designed by the architect John Carr of York, was built between 1780-84. This lithograph from *The Illustrated London News* of 26 August 1854 shows the baths at each end of the Crescent, newly remodelled by Henry Currey, architect to the Duke of Devonshire. The work received quite extensive national coverage, being also fully described in *The Builder* magazine, and was excellent publicity for the emerging Victorian spa.

2. Buxton from Corbar Woods. Dated 12 March 1854, but undoubtedly earlier, this view shows the Crescent, the Great Stables and St John's church. The Wesleyan chapel is visible in the market-place and also shown is the Square. The foreground shows what may be the recently landscaped Corbar Woods. The Crescent is seen from the rear and beyond that the area which was to become known as St Ann's Cliff and, later, 'the Slopes'.

3. Again mistakenly dated 12 March 1854, this view of Bakewell Road (Spring Gardens) does not show the *Royal Hotel* which was completed in 1852. One of the buildings behind the central clump of trees could possibly be the *Angel Hotel*, which was demolished in 1849 to make way for the *Royal Hotel*. This view from Fairfield Hill before any houses were built on Fairfield Road, gives an impression of the pastoral approach to Buxton at that time.

4. Side view of the Crescent, *c.*1840. At this time the Crescent was completely enclosed and the entrance shown here was opposite the *Grove Hotel*, the area being known as Irongate. The roof of the first hot baths may be seen below right; these were built by Charles Sylvester of Derby in 1818. The Crescent wall was taken down in the early 1850s.

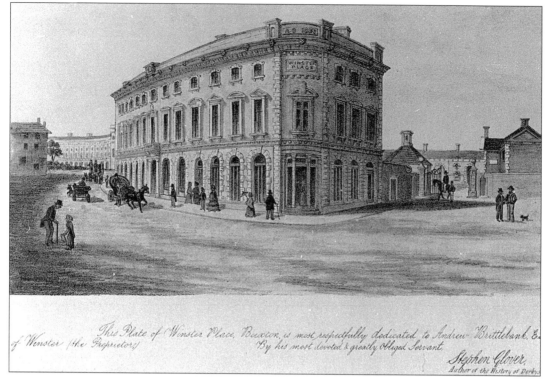

This Plate of Winster Place, Buxton, is most respectfully dedicated to Andrew Brittlebank, Esq. of Winster (the Proprietor). By his most devoted & greatly obliged Servant, Stephen Glover, Author of the History of Derbys

5. The *Royal Hotel* was built between 1849 and 1852 on the site of a previous hotel, the *Angel*. The architect was Samuel Worth of Sheffield and the building was erected under the superintendence of Robert R. Duke. The main financier of the project was Andrew Brittlebank of Winster, hence the name 'Winster Place' carved in the stonework above the eastern corner. In 1914 the building was taken over by the Buxton Lime Firms Co. and became known as the Royal Exchange.

6. An 1854 engraving of the market-place as seen from today's Town Hall. The building on the extreme right of the picture is Buxton College and the larger building to the left of the school is the *Eagle Hotel*. Seen in the distance on the hill is the original 'Solomon's Temple'. The market cross was erected in the position shown in 1813 and was moved to its present site *c.*1947. The four-storeyed block on the left was the *White Hart* inn. The building seen on the extreme left edge was part of Dunmore Square, which was demolished in 1876.

7. Higher Buxton around 1854 looking northwards along High Street from the bottom of London Road. The road to the left is West Street and on the corner, behind the horse and cart, was the Dog Leach pond which was an early source of public water supply. St Anne's church can be seen roughly in the centre of the picture. There is no right junction on this view as Dale Street was yet to be built.

8. Natural Baths after the rebuild of 1850-54 from a print in Dr. Robertson's *Buxton Guide*, first published in 1854. The Natural Baths were built close to or over the sources of the thermal water emerging at a constant 82 degrees Fahrenheit. The effects of the gases arising from it were considered important factors in the healing properties of the water. The fluted niches in the elevation contained fountains and the entrance was in the Crescent arcade close to the mineral and chalybeate water drinking wells.

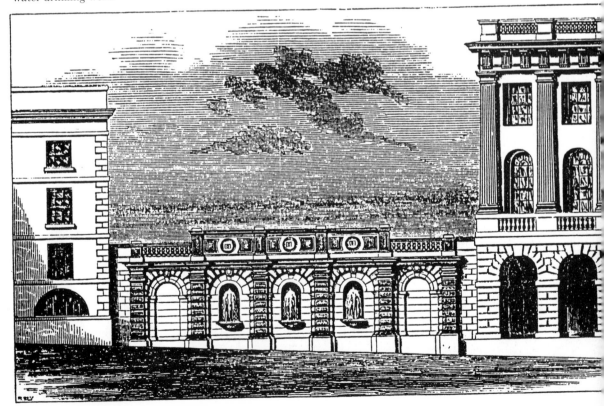

9. A contemporary painting of the 1854 Hot Baths highlighting the splendid façade, described as 'Crystal Palace' style of architecture and capturing the air of Victorian splendour. A copy of this painting can be seen in the Hot Baths building which is now the Cavendish Shopping Arcade.

10. A rare photograph by B. W. Bentley, dated 1858, of the glass and iron colonnaded Hot Baths. Its many bathing facilities included a large cold swimmimg bath which was in the building jutting out to the right. Note behind the baths 'the Quadrant', a curved development of shops and apartments which was begun in 1853 and had grown by this time to eight properties.

11. Poole's Cavern was a popular tourist attraction for hundreds of years. When lit by gas *c.*1860 the laying of the cast-iron supply pipe from the gas-works on Bridge Street was an engineering feat of which the cave's proprietors were justifiably proud, according to contemporary advertisements. The building on the right is the lodge, designed by local architect, R. R. Duke in 1852.

12. In the centre is Buxton's Market Hall, built in 1857 by the partnership of Samuel Turner and R. R. Duke. As the name suggests, the hall was originally used for the sale of market produce, but in later years it seems that trade in meat, fish and fruit dwindled and many of the shops began to sell spar ornaments and souvenirs. The hall burnt down in 1885 and was replaced in 1889 by the present Town Hall.

3. Hardwick Street, shown here in the foreground, off Spring Gardens, was one of the earliest Victorian streets to be developed, commencing in about 1857. The building firm of R. R. Duke carried out much of the road laying and drainage, and by 1860 it was adopted by the Local Board. By 1861 there were eight occupied properties plus three building plots owned by R. R. Duke. The plot in the foreground was to become Milligan's, the well-known Buxton drapers.

4. Congregational church, Hardwick Mount, designed by Henry Currey and built by the firm of R. R. Duke at a cost of £2,725, and opened in 1861. The church was strongly promoted by Robert Broome, wealthy townsman who had interests in limeworks and the Cromford & High Peak Railway. The church was demolished in 1983.

15.   Broadwalk, originally known as Cavendish Terrace, was developed from 1861 to become one of the most fashionable Victorian terraces in the town in its unrivalled position overlooking the pleasure gardens and pavilion. The first three houses built were at the eastern end and known as Cavendish Villas. They were erected for Mr. Barnard, wine and spirit merchant and local politician.

16.   Later view of Broadwalk. The walk was very popular with visitors and most of the villas offered private lodging facilities. It also provided a flat perambulation for the invalid. It is still a fine walk and most of the solid and well-designed villas remain as very good examples of Victorian architecture.

7. An interesting photograph of the London and North Western station, the façade of which remains today. The two railway companies opened their lines to Buxton on the same day, Saturday 30 May 1863. The Midland ran from Rowsley and the L.N.W.R. south from Whaley Bridge. Disagreement between the two companies over station design led to a compromise, proposed by Sir Joseph Paxton (who was himself a director of the Midland Railway Company), resulting in the Midland having a similar façade to that shown here.

18. This 1878 plan of the two stations clearly shows the internal layouts from which it can be seen that the L.N.W.R. offered first and second class waiting room facilities whilst the M.R. offered first and third class. The distinction at that time was rather important! The stations were approached through a central gateway.

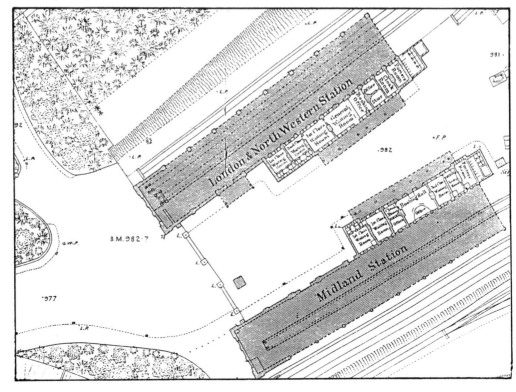

19. Exterior of the L.N.W.R. station taken in 1937 by which time it had become the L.M.S. Western station. The railway services to Buxton in Victorian times were a major lifeline to the town and contributed greatly to its prosperity. In 1891 a tourist ticket from Manchester to Buxton by L.N.W.R. was 7s. 6d., first class; 4s. 8d., second class; and 3s. 11d., third class.

20. The Midland Railway ran from Derby to Buxton through spectacular scenery. This photograph shows Monsal viaduct midway between Bakewell and Buxton. The social critic, John Ruskin was not impressed with the routing of this railway, however, and in the 1860s he wrote in respect of Monsal Dale 'that valley where you might expect to catch the sight of Pan, Apollo and the muses, is now desecrated in order that a Buxton fool may be able to find himself in Bakewell at the end of twelve minutes'.

21.   The *Leewood Hotel*. This hotel, which stands on land between Manchester Road and the Park Ring, was opened in 1864 by Brian Bates who also ran the *Old Hall* and *Royal* hotels at the time. It was described as 'Large and handsome, converted from three private houses ...'. In the 1880s it became popular with 'men of science and letters' and also a place of permanent residence, which was unusual at that time. It is said that a businessman engaged in the chemical industry in Manchester came for a fortnight and eventually died there after being in residence for 25 years!

22.   Buxton, *c*.1863, seen from Corbar Woods. Compared with the earlier engraving (Plate 2), there is a considerable amount of development. Much of Broadwalk is now in existence and Athelstane Terrace on Manchester Road, reputedly designed by Joseph Paxton, is visible on the right of the picture. The trees which were newly planted in the earlier view are now well developed.

23. This building was originally the *Seven Stars Inn*, on High Street (opposite the present *Sun Inn*) which
was enlarged to the designs of R. R. Duke in 1864 when two new dining and refreshment rooms were
added. By 1878 it had been renamed the *Dog and Partridge*. At the time of this photograph (*c.*1928) it was
Gray's ironmonger's shop and it is today occupied by a firm of insurance brokers.

4. *Palace Hotel* depicted on a range of letterheads from 1870 to 1905. The original building was designed by Henry Currey, architect to the Duke of Devonshire, and built between 1864-66. Built as a speculative venture and originally known as the *Buxton Hotel*, it had a precarious start to life but after being bought at auction in 1867 by a re-formed investment company it went on to become Buxton's foremost hotel. R. R. Duke was the clerk of works for the building and also became the first company secretary.

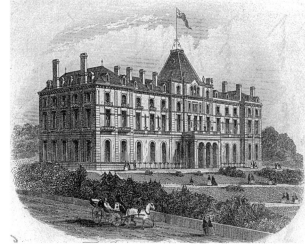

5. *Palace Hotel*. In 1887 the north and west wings were added including a ballroom and dining hall, all designed by R. R. Duke. The *Palace* was frequented by many titled visitors during the season and was promoted by the L.N.W.R. whose directors had substantial shareholdings in the hotel company. It is still used as a hotel, owned by the Forte group, and is the only remaining hotel of the four largest in the town of Edwardian days.

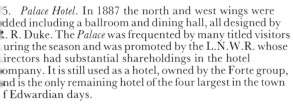

26. An early photograph of St James's church built in 1870/71 to the designs of M. H. Taylor. An impressive building both inside and out, it was intended to provide for the increasing population. The church was demolished in the early 1960s to be replaced by a health centre. Note the limited development of Bath Road in the early 1870s; the houses at the top were the first to be built and may date to the 1860s, but Bath Street, as it was then called, did not emerge fully until the mid-1870s.

27. A rare view from the top of Bath Road showing the demolition of the spire on St James's church, c.1896, for reasons of safety.

28. Pavilion Gardens. The Buxton Improvements Company commissioned the building of a 'winter garden' on 12 acres of land donated by the 7th Duke of Devonshire which had previously been gardens to Buxton Hall. The building was designed by Edward Milner and was opened on 11 May 1871. The gardens and ornamental bridges were designed and set out by Milner's son, Henry. Edward Milner had been a student of Paxton and had assisted in the rebuilding of the Crystal Palace at Sydenham after the Great Exhibition of 1851, and this picture clearly shows its influence.

29. Interior view of the Pavilion Central Hall showing the pipe organ on the right. The town band used to perform concerts in the hall which became a very popular attraction at the Gardens. The original Central Hall burnt down in 1983 and was rebuilt complete with a reproduction cylindrical spire approximating the original of 1871. It is now used as a restaurant.

30.   The Concert Hall built on the western end of the Pavilion building on the site of a former Dutch Garden was designed
by R. R. Duke and opened to the public in August 1876. The extension was commissioned by the Buxton Improvements
Company in order to cope with the growing audiences who attended the popular musical concerts which had previously
been held in the Pavilion Central Hall.

BUXTON IMPROVEMENTS COMPANY
LIMITED.

OPENING

OF THE

NEW CONCERT HALL,

BUXTON GARDENS,

By His Grace the DUKE of DEVONSHIRE, K.G.

ON WEDNESDAY, AUGUST 30th, 1876.

PROGRAMME FOR THE DAY:

FROM 11 A.M. TO 12.45.

Mr. Julian Adams' Brass Band will perform.

AT 12.50 P.M.

THE DIRECTORS RECEIVE HIS GRACE THE

Duke of Devonshire

At the Gates and INSPECT

THE NEW GROUNDS, SKATING RINK, ETC.

Band of King's Dragoon Guards

To Perform during the progress.

AT 1.15 P.M., THE

New Concert Hall

WILL BE

DECLARED OPEN

BY HIS GRACE THE

DUKE OF DEVONSHIRE.

AT 1.30 P.M.

Guards' Band

IN THE CONCERT HALL.

AT 1.30 P.M.

PUBLIC LUNCHEON

IN THE PAVILION.

Tickets: Ladies, 5s; Gentlemen, 7s. 6d. each.

AT 3 P.M.

GUARDS' BAND

IN THE GROUNDS.

Programme:

GRAND MARCH	"Athalie"	MENDELSSOHN.
OVERTURE	"Zampa"	HEROLD.
WALTZ	"Giestes Sewingen"	LANNER.
SELECTION	"Il Pianto Magico"	MOZART.
MAZURKA	"Silks and Satins"	FAUST.
WALTZ	"Doctrinen"	STRAUSS.
SYMPHONY	"Surprise"	HAYDN.
SELECTION	"Scotch Songs"	CAVALLINI.
GALOP (vocal)	"Queen Victoria"	HECKER.

GOD SAVE THE QUEEN.

W. ORTON, Bandmaster.

AT 6.30 P.M., AN

ORCHESTRAL CONCERT

IN THE NEW CONCERT HALL.

Mr. Julian Adams' Band Specially Augmented for the occasion.

Programme:

OVERTURE............"Ruy Blas"............MENDELSSOHN.
VALSE DE CONCERT—"Feuilles du Martin" (Morgenblatter)..
STRAUSS.
SOLO VIOLIN......"Lucrezia Borgia"..............SAINTON.
Miss BERTHA BROUSIL.
GRAND SELECTION...."I Lombardi"............VERDI.
SOLO INSTRUMENTALISTS: Violin, Mr. E. Flexney; Oboe, Mr. C.
Reynolds; Cornet, Mr. Dowling; Euphonium, Mr. S. Moss;
Clarionet, Mr. Green; Trombone, Mr. Silvester; Flute, Mr. Packer, &c.

PART II.

OVERTURE............"William Tell"............ROSSINI.
DUET CONCERTANTE—Piano & Violin..THALBERG & DE BERIOT.
Mr. JULIAN ADAMS and Miss BERTHA BROUSIL.
SOLO HAUTBOIS.."Lur, Linda di Chamóunix"....S. VERROUST.
Mr. CHARLES REYNOLDS.
VALSE DE CONCERT..."La Manolo"........E. WALDTENFEL.
GRAND MARCH....From "Lohengrin" (requested)...WAGNER.

AT 8.30 P.M., A GRAND

Display of Fireworks!

By Messrs. Brock & Co., of the Crystal Palace, London,
consisting of a Splendid Exhibition of

Aquatic Fireworks on the Lake and River	Cascade of Golden Fire
	Set Pieces
Magnesium Balloons	Devices in Words
Special Illumination of the Gardens by Large Coloured Lights	Lance Work Pieces, &c., &c.
Monstre Crystal Palace Shells	Chinese and Japanese Lanterns, &c.

Mr. Julian Adams' Brass Band will play in the Grounds during the Fireworks.

Day Admission to the Grounds by Ticket, 1s.

J. C. BATES, PRINTER, "ADVERTISER" OFFICE, BUXTON.

31. Programme for the opening of the new Concert Hall (now more commonly called the Octagon) in the Pavilion Gardens. All went to plan with the exception of the grand display of fireworks which had to be abandoned due to rain. Earlier fears about the acoustics in the new hall were quickly dispelled by the soloists and musicians who performed on the day.

32. The new Concert Hall from the west. The extension to the left of the building was the board room which was used for meetings of the Buxton Improvements Company. Further left still, and off this picture, was the smoking room. The iron columns supporting the interior and exterior of the building were made and fitted by the Liverpool firm of Rankin and Son who were later to supply the metalwork for the dome on the Devonshire Hospital. As recently as 1967 the local council were contemplating demolishing this building but fortunately the threat was not carried out and it remains for us to appreciate today.

33. Interior of the Concert Hall. Seating was available for 1,000 people. Note the roof windows which helped to light the hall. The dome roof has recently been reslated and the roof windows replaced, but a false ceiling, which was introduced some years ago, prevents the windows lighting the hall as was originally intended.

.   Pavilion Gardens Rink. Opened in 1876, the skating rink stood on land now used for the Pavilion Gardens car park. he north-west corner of the rink was covered over for use during wet weather. In later years the rink was flooded during e winter months and was used for ice-skating and curling.

35. This view of Pavilion Gardens, the bandstand and bridge was captured in 1872 by the famous Buxton photographer B. W. Bentley for an album of 45 views which received national acclaim from the art critics. B. W. Bentley had studios at the Quadrant and Eagle Parade, Buxton and also in Manchester. The ornamental bridge was designed by Henry Milner.

36. Composite map of 1878 showing the layout of the Pavilion and part of the gardens and walks, kept in fine order by Adam Hogg, the curator. The long promenade for use in inclement weather can be clearly seen; also note the group of glasshouses to the left of the Central Hall and the space around the Pavilion before the additions of the Playhouse and Opera House.

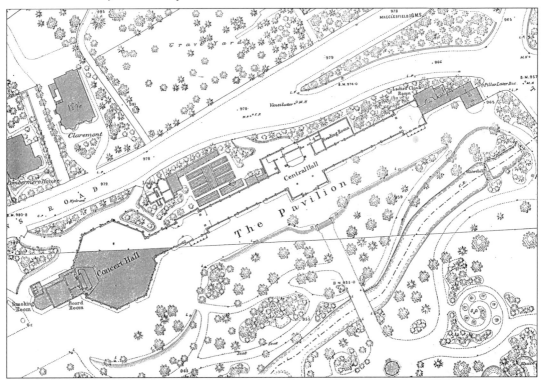

37.   Devonshire Park Wesleyan chapel built in 1873 on the corner of Devonshire Road and Marlborough Road and designed by Mellor & Sutton of Southport. It boasted an octagonal spire and internally it had a rear gallery above a nave which led to an apsidal chancel. It closed in 1918 and was sold to the Christian Science Church in 1925. It was demolished in 1969/70 to make way for housing.

38.   Devonshire Park, shown here in the mid-1870s, was one of the earliest of the fashionable Victorian developments in Buxton. Substantial villa properties were built from the late 1860s and the present Marlborough Road and Devonshire Road were laid out. Many of the houses remain today, though most are converted into flats.

39. An unusual and rarely seen view of the area known to Buxtonians as 'Sparrow Park' to the south of Hardwick Street. The sloping grass area shown in this c.1876 view now has trees. It has been used as Buxton's equivalent to Hyde Park's speaker's corner with local lay-preachers and politicians taking to their soapboxes. Trinity church is seen at the top right of the picture.

40. Trinity church was built in 1873 to the designs of R. R. Duke. The church, at the top of Hardwick Mount, was extended by the addition of a new transept in 1883 and a tower in 1906. The prime mover in its origins and early growth was the solicitor J. W. Taylor, who was the senior trustee for 50 years and a prominent townsman.

1. A Buxton winter, *c*.1875. The *Old Hall Hotel* to the left, the Natural Baths in the centre and *St Ann's Hotel* to the right.
ehind these is the Devonshire Hospital when it operated as part hospital, part stables, well before the addition of the
omed roof. Beyond the hospital Devonshire Park is being developed with fashionable houses.

42. A view of the bottom of Terrace Road in the 1870s. The building on the corner of Terrace Road and Spring Gardens is Lawson's Wine Vaults. Slightly further up the road is Oram's fishmonger's shop and further still is Flint's confectioner's. Lawson's corner, as it was known, projected into Spring Gardens and was demolished under an order of 1876. The same order authorised the demolition of Dunmore Square on the market-place.

43. A rare photograph of Buxton market-place in the 1870s showing the buildings at the side of the *Eagle Hotel* which were replaced by Eagle Parade in 1890. The middle building with the pointed frontage was the Buxton College schoolhouse which operated at this site until 1867. Beyond the schoolhouse were the premises of B. W. Bentley the photographer. The two shops shown are Rowland Brothers, grocers, and Hargreaves and Son, china and glass merchants. The china business of Hargreaves and Son still trades from premises in Spring Gardens.

4. An unusual view of the side of the Market Hall taken by B. W. Bentley in the early 1870s. The buildings on the right were a continuation of Belmont Terrace known as St Ann's Square. The board over no. 2 is of T. J. Stevenson, auctioneer, grocer and private lodging house. A hard-working man, he was also Inspector of Nuisances to the Local Board. Next door was Miss Backhouse, confectioner and, in common with many premises in Buxton, also offering private lodgings.

5. Terrace Road, *c.*1875. On the right is Buxton House which, together with the row of seven cottages below it, were to form the *Buxton House Hydropathic* in the 1880s. On the left is Belmont Terrace, the lower part of which was built in the early 1860s. The wooden tressels on the road sides perhaps indicate that the drainage grids were being improved.

46. London Road Tollbar which stood at the junction of the Brierlow Bar to Buxton and Buxton to Macclesfield turnpike roads. The *London Road Inn*, which is still in use as a public house, can be seen on the right. The tollbar stood on, or near to, the land now occupied by the petrol station at the bottom of London Road.

47. Lower Buxton. This photograph was donated to the Buxton Museum by Mrs. Aston Smith, daughter of R. R. Duke. It dates to 1876 and the newly-built *Burlington Hotel* can be seen on the left. At this time the terrace walks (known as St Ann's Cliff, and, latterly, 'the Slopes') which were reputedly laid out by Sir Jeffrey Wyatville in 1818 and completed in 1840 by Paxton, were devoid of trees. It is thought that most of the trees were planted after the turn of the century.

48. Randolph Caldecott (1846-86), the celebrated artist and illustrator, spent his early career in banking in Manchester where his drawings were first published, subsequently his cartoons and illustrations appeared in many books, newspapers and magazines including *Punch*. In 1876 he visited Buxton for a health cure and this sketch is taken from one of his letters.

On the 2nd November, 1876, he writes :—

AT BUXTON.

" I am as above. Walking solemnly in the gardens, or sitting limply in the almost deserted saloon listening to an enfeebled band."

49-52. Caldecott's visit resulted in a series of delightful sketches which appeared in the *Graphic* newspaper of 31 March 1877, entitled 'Sketches at Buxton by a rheumatic man'. We do not know how effective his treatment was in Buxton but he died in 1886 at the early age of forty.

The Promenade.

The View from St. Ann's Cliff. —

Meet of the Harrie[rs]

In the Saloon — (Ladies working — Band playing.)

A Cardiac Complication —

An Incorrigible Beau.

"MARCH OF THE MEN OF BUXTON."

Chacun a son goût.

R. Caldecott

53.   Public pump at the base of the Slopes which was in use from 1852-94. One side of the pump delivered ordinary cold spring water and the other thermal water at a temperature of 82 degrees Fahrenheit. The town authorities are still today obliged to maintain a public pump under a directive from the Buxton Enclosure Act of 1772 which decrees that Buxton people must have access to the natural spring water. The house to the right, at the bottom of Hall Bank, was demolished to make way for the *Burlington Hotel*.

54.   *Burlington Hotel*, situated at the foot of Hall Bank. Built in 1874 by Jas Turner, to the designs of R. R. Duke, at a total cost of £4,520.17s , the hotel was later renamed the *Savoy* and was for some time a training hotel for the brewery trade. The building is now private flats.

5. The *Burlington* by 1906, the date of this postcard, had become the *Savoy Hotel*. This view shows the entrance to Hartington Street in the centre of the card. The two-gabled house which can just be seen in the centre is Thorncliffe, designed and built by R. R. Duke in 1862 for J. C. Bates, proprietor of the *Buxton Advertiser*.

56. Burlington Road was commenced in 1876 from St John's Road but was not fully completed until the 1880s. The first houses to be built were called Rockavon and Buckingham and now form the *Buckingham Hotel*. This photograph is taken from the upstairs window of one of the houses in the late 1870s and shows new fashionable housing on St John's Road. In the right foreground can be seen the roof of the skating rink in the Pavilion Gardens.

7. New Charity Hot Baths. By the 1870s the bath facilities had become very busy and in order to make more facilities available the Duke of Devonshire paid for new hot and natural baths to be built for the use of the charity patients of the Devonshire Hospital. These were designed by R. R. Duke. No contemporary picture has come to light but this modern photograph shows the Charity Hot Baths in George Street, built in 1876.

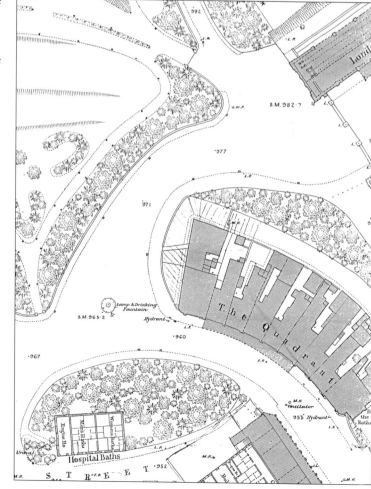

8. This map of 1878 shows the position and layout of the Charity Hot Baths. The men's and women's baths were separated and the water was heated in the engine house on the left. The building still remains on George Street. This plan also shows the three-light fountain designed by R. R. Duke in 1868 situated at the junction of Manchester Road and Station Road. It was criticised by the local newspaper as being 'meanly inadequate to its position'.

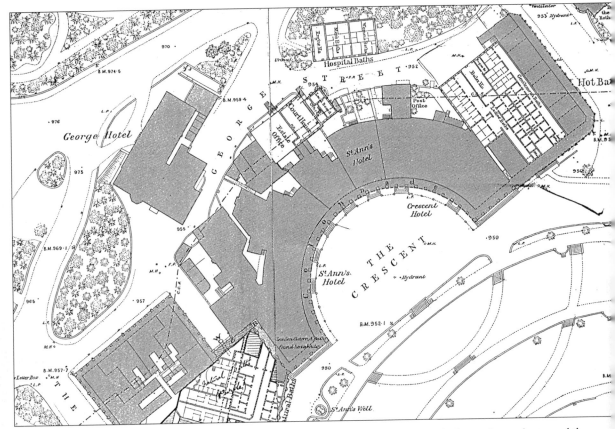

59. A section from the same map showing the internal layout of the Hot and Natural Baths for paying patients, and the relative position of the Charity Hot Baths. Note particularly the possible site of the Roman bath under the west wing of the Crescent. This bath or 'leaden cistern' was last uncovered when the foundations for the Crescent were dug *c.*1780. Also seen at the rear of the Crescent is the Post Office, built in the early 1860s. It was to this office that the first telegraph line was brought.

60. The Charity Natural Baths, also built in 1876, were situated under a roadway leading to the back of the Square. The facilities were much smaller than those previously available and these diminutive baths were entered by the charity patients from the rear of the building so that they did not mix with the paying patients in the main baths building. This picture shows the present-day remains of the baths.

. This seemingly ordinary view is important in the history of Buxton's charity baths. Taken in 1872 by B. W. Bentley, shows the rear entrance to the Natural Baths which was reserved for patients of the Buxton Bath Charity. The doorway just to the right of the arch in the background of the picture. In the foreground is seen the start of the culverted river Wye hich passes under the Square, the Crescent, the Hot Baths and the bottom of the Quadrant. At this time the Wye formed e boundary between the townships of Fairfield and Buxton.

62.   Buxton from Corbar Hill, *c.*1877. The building in the left foreground is the Wesleyan chapel in Devonshire Park before the spire was added. The Devonshire Hospital is clearly seen before the addition of the dome roof. The building was originally The Great Stables, designed by the York architect, John Carr and built in 1789. The 1840 Paxton layout of the paths on St Ann's Cliff can be clearly seen on the left.

63.   Lower Buxton in 1878 showing many of the important buildings including the range of baths, the Devonshire Hospital and the *Palace Hotel*. To the bottom left is the Pavilion and on the right Spring Gardens and Terrace Road. There are no fewer than seven hotels in this area of Buxton.

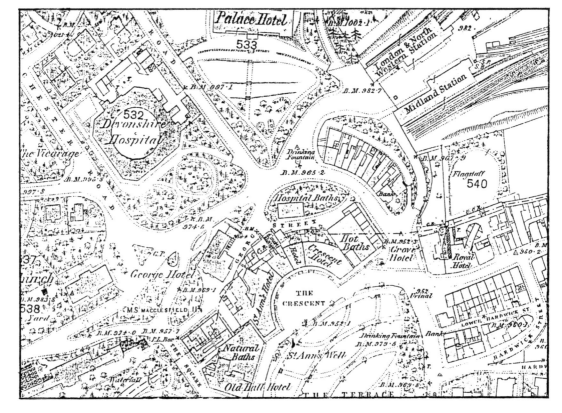

64. Turner's Memorial was erected outside the Hot Baths in 1879. R. R. Duke initiated the subscription for it and the memorial was built to his design in memory of his good friend, Samuel Turner. Turner had been a builder in the town and went on to become a sub-agent at the Devonshire Estate Office for many years. Turner was also a trustee of the Devonshire Hospital, a member of the Local Board, a director of the Buxton Improvements Company and a churchwarden at St John's church for over thirty years.

65. The same memorial after an encounter with a van driven by a local man in 1959. Although it appears from the picture to be only superficially damaged, it was demolished after this incident. Attempts are currently being made to reconstruct the memorial. This closer view of the memorial shows more clearly the drinking bowls which were made of either marble or, possibly, Derbyshire Spar.

Robert R Duke
architect
31 Spring Gro..., Lewe.
1880.

66.   Internal view of the construction of the massive dome at the Devonshire Hospital in 1880, designed by R. R. Duke.
During the conversions much additional work was done in extending the building and converting it to be used exclusively
as a hospital. Prior to this it had been part hospital, part stables. The domed roof was considered an architectural 'tour
de force' and fully described in the technical press of the day.

7. The construction of the giant dome at the Devonshire Hospital, seen from Manchester Road. During this work the architect, R. R. Duke, happened to meet a railway engineer who informed him of design faults in the metalwork which had contributed to the recently fallen Tay Bridge. This caused Duke to go immediately to the hospital and order the redrilling of parts of the supporting ribs of his dome. This and the previous photograph were commissioned and donated to the hospital by R. R. Duke.

8. Plan sketch of the Devonshire Hospital before the extensions were completed in 1881. It had been intended to build a lodge on either side of the main entrance but, despite a donation of £24,000 from the governors of the Cotton Districts Convalescent Fund, the project ran out of money and the left lodge and portico over the entrance were never built.

R.R. DUKE ARCHITECT

69. External view showing the front of the Devonshire Hospital. Included as part of the hospital extensions was a new drinking well room in George Street adjacent to the Charity Hot Baths. It was conceived and designed by R. R. Duke and the building still remains, now housing the pump to supply the Devonshire Royal Hospital with natural mineral water.

70. Postcard showing the interior of the dome. It is 138 ft. across and the wrought-iron ribs supporting the dome consist of 22 principals and 22 intermediates, secured at their base to a wrought-iron ring which prevents the great weight of the dome from pushing apart the supporting stone pillars. These pillars are reputed to have come from the ruins of Bolton Abbey. The ribs rise to a height of 75 ft. from the floor and join at the top a wrought-iron ring 40 ft. in diameter. The dome is topped with a glazed circle in order to light the building.

71. William, the 7th Duke of Devonshire (1808-91), assumed the title in 1858 and with it substantial investments in Buxton. His policy was to encourage a greater degree of self-sufficiency in townspeople by providing new facilities. He also sold much land for building – an action which paid off because of the phenomenal growth and increase in popularity of the inland resort during his time.

72. Chatsworth House, Derbyshire, seat of the Devonshire family. The original house was built in the mid 16th-century by Bess of Hardwick, but it was substantially rebuilt in the late 17th and early 18th centuries by William, the 4th Earl (1st Duke) of Devonshire. Successive dukes extended the house, gardens and the collections of books and art treasures. William Spencer, the 6th Duke, who did much to influence the growth of Buxton, wrote a handbook describing Chatsworth and its many rooms.

73. George Drewry was the Duke of Devonshire's Buxton Agent from 1864-78 when his son, Frank, took over the position until 1919. Because of the estate's extensive holdings in the town, the Duke's agents exerted a very powerful influence on its development throughout the Victorian era. Very little happened which did not go through the Estate Office in George Street.

74. Though resident at the Duke of Devonshire's estate at Holker, George Drewry continued to influence developments at Buxton. Here he writes to Frank regarding the proposed new pump room. His letter is significant in that he is asking for plans drawn up by R. R. Duke in preference to those of the Devonshire estate's own architect, Henry Currey. Although the pump room of 1894 was ultimately to Currey's design there is no doubt that R. R. Duke had some measure of involvement in it.

Holker
Cartle-in-Cartmel
Camforth.
June 28th 1891.

My Dear Frank,

Lord Hartington & Lady Louisa examined Mr Currey's Plan of the Pumproom and I do not think they quite like it.

I believe Mr Duke has a plan for one. If so let me have it by return of Post and also send me a Photograph of the Crescent and the Slopes. — — — — —
— — — — —

Your aff Father
Geo Drewry

Dr. W. H. Robertson, long-serving chairman of trustees and senior physician of the Devonshire Hospital. Robertson was one of the most influential figures in the development of Victorian Buxton and an authority on water treatment. He published several books including the *Guide to the Use of Buxton Waters* in 1838 and the much reprinted *Guide to Buxton and the Peak of Derbyshire*. He served as Chairman of the Buxton Improvements Company while the Pavilion Gardens was being developed.

Dr. Robertson chaired the Devonshire Hospital trustees throughout the whole period of the gradual conversion of the building from stables to hospital. During the extensions of 1881 a clock tower, paid for by public subscription, was erected on the east of the building as a testimonial to him. The clock, which chimes the quarters and has four faces, was given by the 7th Duke of Devonshire. This view of hospital patients also shows the statue of the 7th Duke in the centre of the hospital which was actually the plaster original from which a bronze was cast and erected at Eastbourne.

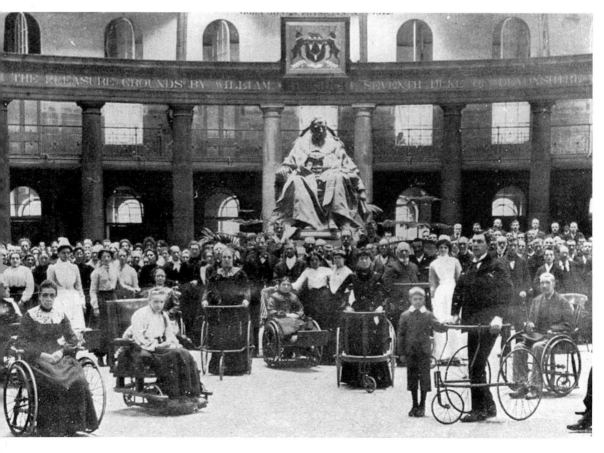

77. *(above left)* Robert Rippon Duke, the builder/architect who came to Buxton for his health's sake and lived to the age of 92! His was the classic rise through Victorian society from joiner, self-taught draughtsman, builder, surveyor to full-blown architect. He was innovative in his designs and not afraid to take risks with new materials and techniques. He became involved in many activities in the town and was, notably, a long-serving member of the Devonshire Hospital trustees including a period as chairman.

78. *(above)* As Architect and Surveyor to the Devonshire Buxton estate for almost 40 years, as well as an architect in private practice, R. R. Duke's influence was widespread and detailed. In addition to his own designs he advised on many of the new properties built upon land sold by the Devonshire Estate. He also laid out no less than 34 new roads in the town. Many examples of his work are shown in this book.

79. *(left)* Josiah Taylor was the first Clerk to the Local Board formed in 1859 and he served through the Urban District Council to become the first Town Clerk of the newly-formed Buxton Borough in 1917. He was made the first freeman of the borough in 1918 and retired in 1919. His 60 years' service as a chief officer must be unparalleled in local government service.

80. The Town Hall was designed by William Pollard and opened in 1889. It was built of local stone and by a local builder, James Salt. Originally the building had open arcades on either side as seen in this photograph. The Local Board offices were previously in George Street, adjacent to the Court House. A former 'town hall', situated on the market-place, had for some time been considered inadequate for the growing town.

81. Rear or northern aspect of the Town Hall which overlooks the Slopes and presents a façade as equally imposing as the front. The two men standing on the stone ledge over the doorway appear to be posing somewhat precariously for the camera! Note the use of weathered limestone, which was quarried locally and used in rockery arrangements.

82. Edward Chambers Milligan was a well-known townsman, member of the Local Board for many years, and also a member of the Devonshire Hospital management committee. He has been described as the leading draper in the town who dressed immaculately for business in frock-coat, striped trousers and patent leather shoes.

83. Milligan's drapery shop with its elegant Edwardian glass verandah on the corner of Spring Gardens and Hardwick Street. The business was founded by John Milligan in 1846 and was passed on to his son, Edward, in 1871. The shop was originally in Spring Gardens, opposite the *Shakespeare Hotel*. The business later moved to Winster Place and from there to Hardwick Street. (Plate 13 shows the site cleared ready for the erection of this building.)

4. The centre foreground of this picture shows the Post Office in Cavendish Circus which was designed by R. R. Duke and built in 1881. The Post Office was previously situated behind the Crescent. On the left, the Quadrant, which was built progressively during the 1850s with a common architectural style for each addition, curves round towards Spring Gardens. The Post Office moved to the Quadrant, its present site, in 1905.

85. Buxton College built in 1881. The school has a long history extending at least as far back as 1674. The original school was next to St Anne's Anglican church. It was placed in chancery between 1791-1816 and reopened in the disused St Anne's church. In 1840 it was moved to premises on the market-place (see Plate 6) and in 1867 to the corner of Market Street and South Street. It became a grammar school in 1923 and has recently been greatly extended and renamed Buxton Community School.

86. This photograph by B. W. Bentley was taken from the dome of the Devonshire Hospital and shows, in the centre, the Union Club when newly built in 1886. It was designed by W. R. Bryden (who took over the business of R. R. Duke on his retirement) and offered a non-political gentlemen's club for use by residents and visitors.

87. The Hippodrome was opened in 1889 and designed by architect W. R. Bryden. The town had been without a theatre since the demolition of the Hall Bank theatre in 1854. It was originally called the Entertainment Stage, then the New Theatre; later still, it became a cinema, the Hippodrome, and in about 1934 it was restored to a theatre and renamed the Playhouse. It is no longer used as a theatre but forms part of the Pavilion Gardens complex known as the 'Paxton Suite'.

⇥ PAVILION THEATRE, BUXTON. ⇤

Manager · · · · · Mr. J. WILLOUGHBY.

Monday, Oct. 5, 1896, For Three Nights Only.

SPECIAL ENGAGEMENT OF

Mr. W. S. Penley's London Company

IN THE SUCCESSFUL LIGHT COMEDY,

Jedbury Junior,

By MADELINE LUCETTE RYLEY.

CHRISTOPHER JEDBURY, Junr.	Mr. ALEXANDER BRADLEY
CHRISTOPHER JEDBURY, Senr.	Mr. LESLIE NORMAN
Major HEDWAY	Mr. FRANCIS HAWLEY
TOM BELLABY	Mr. HERBERT COLVILLE
Mr. GLIBB	Mr. GRAHAME HERINGTON
Mr. SIMPSON	Mr. GUY MASSON
WHIMPER	Mr. W. DEVEREUX
JOB	Mr. J. G. DAVIS
Mrs. JEDBURY	Miss ILEENE HOWARD
Mrs. GLIBB	Miss EDITH GORDON
NELLIE JEDBURY	Miss ZOE DAVIS
DORA HEDWAY	Miss ANNIE AUMONIER

ACT 1. ... ... **Jedbury Junr.'s Rooms in Jermyn Street**

The Grey Dove.

A WEEK ELAPSES.

ACT 2. ... ... **The Inner Hall at Blewerton Court**

Mr. Jedbury's House in Devonshire.   The First Waltz.

SIX MONTHS ELAPSE.

ACT 3. ... ... **Major Hedway's Bungalow at Bombay**

What's Bred in the Bone comes out in the Flesh.

SIX WEEKS ELAPSE.

ACT 4. ... ... **Major Hedway's Bungalow at Bombay**

All's Well that Ends Well.

ACTING MANAGER		.... Mr. GUY MASSON
STAGE MANAGER	For	.... Mr. FRANCIS HAWLEY
ADVANCE REPRESENTATIVE	Mr. W. S. PENLEY.	.... Mr. WILLIAM BENSON
MASTER CARPENTER		.... Mr. ALFRED PENNETT

PRICES :—Reserved Seats, 3s.; Second Seats, 2s.; Balcony, 1s. 6d.; Back Seats, 1s.

Doors Open at 7.30, Commence at 8.

October 12, 13, 14.—Roberts, Archer, and Bartlett's Company, in "THE MAGISTRATE."

Advertiser and List of Visitors Offices, Market Place, Buxton.

88. An early example of a programme for the Pavilion (or New) Theatre.

9. By the mid-1880s the hydropathic movement was gaining popularity in the town. The *Peak Hydro*, established in 1880 s *Buxton House Hydropathic* by Dr. Samuel Hyde, had a chequered history. Early building investment ran into difficulties ut by 1885 several new wings and the impressive frontage had been added. It was renamed the *Peak Hydropathic stablishment* in 1887 and was further extended, though by 1915 it had been sold several times and repossessed by the Leek & Moorlands Building Society on two occasions. Part of the building now houses the Buxton Museum and Art Gallery.

The *Peak Hydropathic* in its yday, this advertisement tes from 1900. A source of ter was discovered at this dro though it was a cold ing. However, it was ficient for Dr. Hyde, the oprietor, to engage in a otracted legal argument when felt that the Act of rliament for the ablishment of the new pump m in the Crescent might ny him the use of his own ter source.

THE PEAK HYDRO,
BUXTON.

Summer Tariff.

Board and Lodging, taking meals at Table d'Hôte, from June 1st to September 30th— 8/- to 12/- per day, according to position of Bedroom.

Telegrams:—"Peak, Buxton." Telephone No. 11.

Winter Tariff.

Board and Lodging from October 1st to May 31st (except Easter and Whitsuntide)— 7/- per day, including Baths. Special Rooms extra.

Telegrams:—"Peak, Buxton." Telephone No. 11.

The Hydro is splendidly situated : close to the Stations, Public Baths, and Gardens. It contains 120 Bed and Sitting Rooms, magnificent Drawing Room, Billiard and Smoke Rooms. The **Recreation Room** (recently erected under the supervision of an eminent architect) is the finest in the district. Concerts, Entertainments, Dances, &c., are regularly held. **Assemblies** are held on the first Saturday in the month during the Winter.

Special attention is paid to the Cuisine. Table d'Hôte at separate tables, 6-45 p.m.

The Establishment has no Excise License, but visitors may provide their own Wines. For further particulars apply

THE MANAGERESS, THE PEAK HYDRO, BUXTON.

The Lounge.   Telephone No. 4.   Telegrams: "Haddon Hall, Buxton."

The Dining Room.

HADDON HALL HYDRO, Buxton.

—— OPENED IN 1903.——
ESTABLISHED 30 YEARS.

The only Hydro in Buxton with Tennis Court and Bowling Green

Built on the latest and most approved sanitary principles.

Occupies a commanding position 1,200 feet above sea level.

Every modern comfort.

Electric, Nauheim and Hydropathic Baths, with installations on the most approved principle.

Massage.

Tennis, Bowls, Quoits, Golf, Boating, Hunting, Fishing, etc., all within easy reach.

Booklet free on application to the Manager.

Efficient Postal and Telegraph service

91. Advertisement for the *Haddon Hall Hydro* on London Road, behind which was the *Haddon Grove Hydro*. The *Haddon Grove* was renamed *Oliver's Hydro* and run by the Oliver family who acquired the *Haddon Hall* and renamed the whole complex *Oliver's Haddon Hall Hydro*. In more recent times the building was known as the Electricity Hall and was used as a training centre for the Electricity Board. Nowadays it is a private hotel and retains the name of *Haddon Hall*. The earlier name of *Haddon Grove* can still be seen inscribed in the low wall at the front of the building

The Clarendon
BUXTON.

(*Corbar Hill Hydropathic Ltd.*)

※※※

IS pleasantly situated on the Manchester Road within five minutes' walk of the famous Thermal Baths and Wells, the Public Gardens, Opera House and Railway Stations.

The Clarendon faces the south-west, and the temperature has been regulated so as to make it suitable for a winter, as well as a summer residence.

Electric Light.   **New Lounge.**

Special Terms for Winter, for Long Residence, and for Week-end Visitors.   *Apply Manageress.*

NATIONAL TELEPHONE No. 3.

10

92. Advertisement for the *Clarendon*. It is reputed that a Roman bath was discovered in the land to the rear of this property *c*.1880, but firm evidence for this is scarce. Originally called *Corbar Hill House*, it was used as a home for the treatment of alcoholics. It later became a hydropathic establishment and was sold in 1931 to be used as nurses' accommodation for the Devonshire Hospital. It is currently used as offices and is physically connected to the hospital.

3. *Malvern House Hydropathic Hotel* was one of the town's first lodging houses to offer hydropathy (cold water treatments) in the premises. Opened in 1866 in one of a block of four town houses, it eventually took over the whole block and in 1899 was substantially enlarged and renamed the *Buxton Hydropathic Ltd*. It was a very successful venture in a highly competitive field and, at the turn of the 19th century, dances and other events held there received regular coverage in the local newspapers.

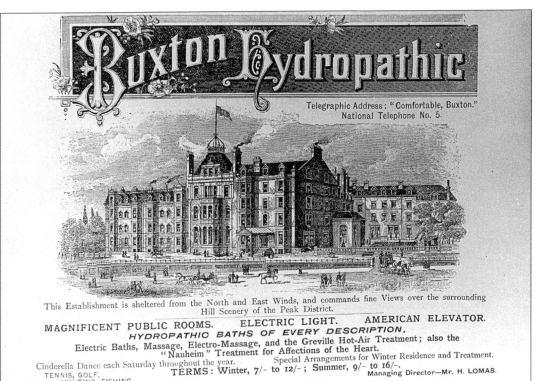

Buxton Hydropathic

Telegraphic Address: "Comfortable, Buxton."
National Telephone No. 5.

This Establishment is sheltered from the North and East Winds, and commands fine Views over the surrounding Hill Scenery of the Peak District.

MAGNIFICENT PUBLIC ROOMS. ELECTRIC LIGHT. AMERICAN ELEVATOR.

HYDROPATHIC BATHS OF EVERY DESCRIPTION,

Electric Baths, Massage, Electro-Massage, and the Greville Hot-Air Treatment; also the "Nauheim" Treatment for Affections of the Heart.

Cinderella Dance each Saturday throughout the year. Special Arrangements for Winter Residence and Treatment.

TENNIS, GOLF, TERMS: Winter, 7/- to 12/-; Summer, 9/- to 16/-.
HUNTING, FISHING. Managing Director—Mr. H. LOMAS.

94. An advertisement from the 1890s illustrating the artistic licence typical of the Victorian entrepreneur. Compare this with a photograph of the actual building in the previous plate. The hydro hit harder times prior to the First World War, after which it became the Granville Military Hospital and subsequently one of the discharge bases for Canadian troops. It was renamed the *Spa Hotel* in 1931, under the continuing management of A. W. Lomas, and was demolished *c*.1975 by the High Peak Borough Council to make room for sheltered flats.

95. The *Spa Hotel* lounge interior is redolent of the spa age and, as the hotel's own publicity says, '... There are no draughts ... there is warmth without stuffiness – ample room for everyone to find their own "pet plots"'.

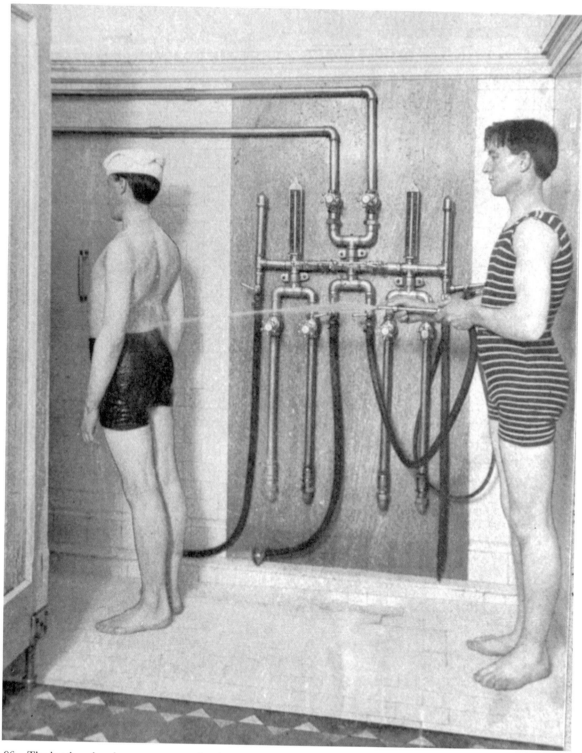

96. The lumbar douche was an example of the type of water treatment on offer at the Buxton baths. Water was sprayed on to the affected area under pressure and was considered beneficial for backache and muscular disorders. A variant of this was the Scottish douche which used two hoses, one hot and the other cold.

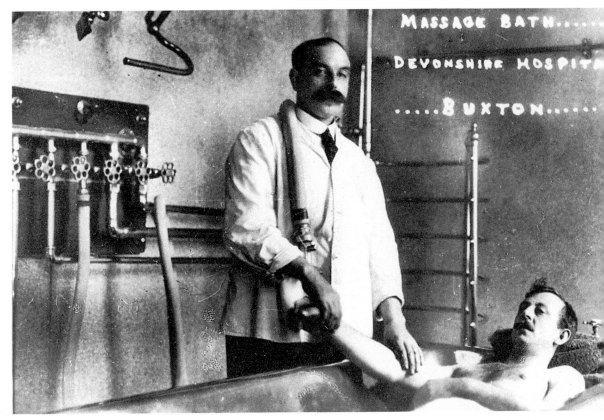

97.   Patient receiving the Buxton douche massage treatment at the Hospital Baths. The patient was laid in the wet bath and was sprayed with thermal water over the length of the body. A variety of rheumatic and arthritic conditions was treated in this way.

98.   The surge bath was an ingenious treatment. It was hydropathic version of the rocking chair and it certain looks a rather precarious, if to say dangerous, form of medical treatment. It is typ of some of the more curiou treatments available in 19t century hydrotherapy, som which, involving the use of electrical currents, must ha been rather dangerous.

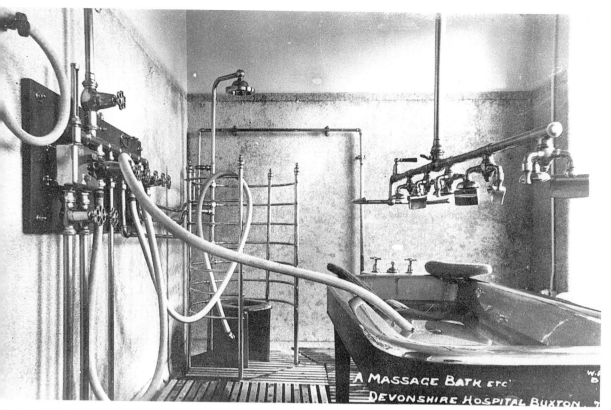

A MASSAGE BATH ETC
DEVONSHIRE HOSPITAL BUXTON

99.   Massage bath at the Devonshire Hospital. In the corner of the room is a piece of apparatus which was used to deliver a conventional shower, a needle bath through small perforations on the inner surface of the concentric horizontal pipes, and the ascending douche which is incorporated in the seat at the bottom of the apparatus.

100.   Treatments on offer at Buxton would have included the splenic douche (left) which involved the localised spraying of a jet of water to the region of the spleen. The vapour douche (right) is a spray of fine water droplets which gives a more diverse application to a larger area of the body.

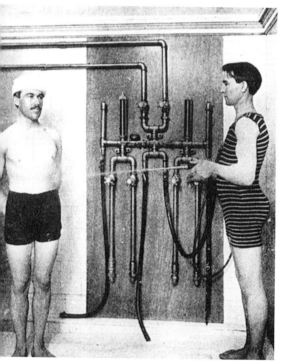

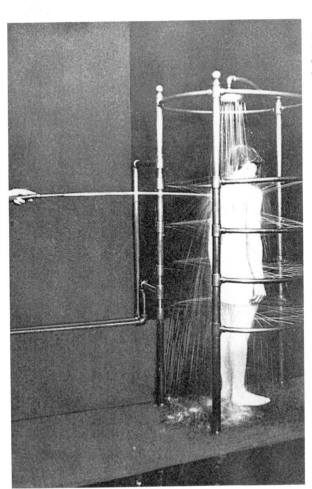

101. This patient is shown receiving three douche baths at the same time. The overhead water spray was known as the rain bath, and the horizontal piping shows the needle bath in operation. In this example the horizontal hand-held jet douche is added for good measure.

At the "Natural Baths."

Attendant: "What is it you are calling for?"

'Enery Horgustus: "I say, look 'ere, where's the bloomin' SOAP? !!

102. A cartoon by W. G. Baxter, 'At the Natural Baths'.

103. Devonshire Hospital immersion bath. This type of bath would have been used in the hospital Charity Baths until 1914 when new baths were built on the south front of the main hospital grounds.

Crochet and Flirtation

An Enviable Invalid

104-109. The cartoonist W. G. Baxter published a series of 50 humorous sketches in a book priced at one shilling. The following are taken from the second edition of *c*.1885 and offer amusing but quite accurate insights into the experiences of the visitors to Buxton. The *Buxton Advertiser* also published his cartoons.

A wet evening. Promenading inside the Pavilion

The Rink

The unfortunate result of an impetuous and short-sighted gent attempting to take a chair.

The Bathchairman afterwards remarked, "that he never met with such a heavy gentleman before."

Taking the waters under difficulties.

110. The Pump Room at 11.00 a.m. This cartoon shows the Pump Room at the Natural Baths before the building of the new Pump Room and, though intended to be humorous, it actually shows how crowded it had become.

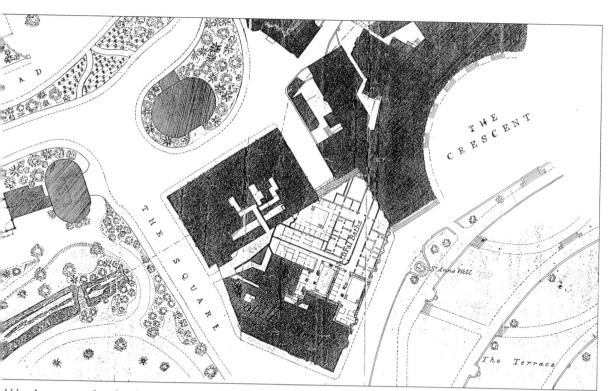

111. A very rare plan showing proposed sites for the new Pump Room. The existing Pump Room at the Natural Baths became overcrowded by the early 1880s and it was decided to build a new one, but there was disagreement as to its site. Two suggestions appear on this plan marked as ovals, one on the spare land to the north of the Square and the other on the site now occupied by the Opera House.

112. The new Pump Room was built in 1893/94 to the designs of the Duke of Devonshire's architect, Henry Currey. It was opened by the 8th Duke and originally had open arcading. This was enclosed in 1911-12 and the pepper pot domes at either end of the building were removed c.1937.

113. Interior of the Pump Room where the famous Buxton thermal water and chalybeate water could be sampled in relaxed setting. Nowadays the Pump Room houses the Micrarium which is a unique exhibition showing many varied plants and creatures specially presented through projection microscopes.

114. The dispensing pool in the Pump Room. Water was pumped to this pool from the springs across the road at the Natural Baths. The pool still exists but is no longer accessible to the public.

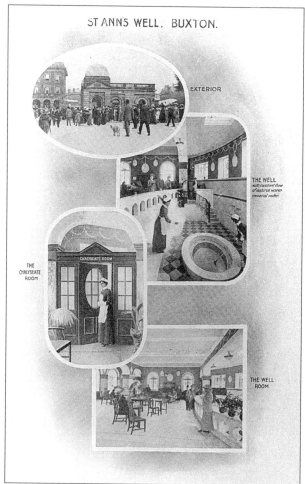

ST ANN'S WELL. BUXTON.

EXTERIOR

THE WELL
with constant flow of natural warm mineral water.

THE CHALYBEATE ROOM

CHALYBEATE ROOM

THE WELL ROOM

5. The Pump Room. A display of facilities in the early 1900s shows a separate room within the building for the dispensing of chalybeate or iron water. The chalybeate water originated from a spring in a band of shale between the junction of Buxton's limestone and gritstone beds. Buxton's chalybeate water was described as mild and was used as a general tonic, as treatment for anaemia and as an eye bath.

116.   The well on Buxton market-place in 1888 decorated for the well-dressing festival. This particular 'well' (which was
actually a pump) remains today and was donated by the Duke of Devonshire to the residents of Higher Buxton in 1840
to provide them with a clean water supply. It is still dressed annually and although the stonework is much eroded the date
1840 can just be deciphered. The pump was fed from a reservoir on Manchester Road.

117. The dressing of wells is a widespread custom in Derbyshire and takes place through the summer. Wells are decorated with flower petals, seeds, mosses and leaves pressed into a clay base to form a scene, normally of a religious nature. Its origins are obscure but likely to be pagan thanksgivings to the water gods, later adopted as a Christian festival. The first recorded well-dressing in Buxton took place in 1840.

118. Three wells are dressed annually in Buxton in July during a week of celebrations. They are situated on the market-place, the Crescent (St Anne's Well) and at the eastern end of Spring Garden (the children's well). The festival includes the well-dressing queen and her entourage. This photograph shows the 1909 queen, Mabel Hyde, with her attendants.

119. The well-dressing festivities include a parade of dressed floats around the town, the arrival of the fair and the decoration of houses and shops. A handsomely decorated float was usually provided for the queen, though this photograph of 1907, taken outside the *Old Hall*, shows a more modest, but nevertheless delightful, mode of transport. The queen is Amy Bagshaw.

20. Buxton from the Town Hall in 1900. The *Old Hall Hotel* is on the left, the Natural Baths and Hot Baths on either side of the Crescent with the Pump Room in the centre. The *Palace Hotel* stands in a commanding position on the right. Note also the Terrace Walks, or Slopes, which provided gradually more challenging gradients for the improving invalid.

121.   In Victorian times public gardens provided a popular form of recreation. Buxton had its own fine examples of this Victorian 'gardenesque', none more so than the Pavilion Gardens where extensive walks and promenades were developed. This view shows the main terrace in front of the glass and iron pavilion buildings. Beyond the domed Concert Hall was a smoking room and directors' room on the site of which now stands the public swimming baths begun by the architect J. Poulson in 1969 and completed in 1972.

122.   A view of the Pavilion Gardens, showing in the foreground one of the ornamental waterfalls designed by Henry Milner, son of the designer of the Pavilion, Edward Milner. Henry Milner published papers on the art and practice of landscape gardening, including a detailed description and plan of the Buxton Gardens.

123. A delightful photograph of 1900 showing Victorian children feeding the pigeons in the Pavilion Gardens. A large decorative flower urn typical of the garden's decorations is in the centre and the large Concert Hall may be seen in the background.

124.   Serpentine Walks. The day-to-day supervision of the Pavilion Gardens was in the capable hands of curator, Adam Hogg. The winding nature of the river Wye allowed for the design and upkeep of very attractive walks.

5.   The refreshment kiosk at the Pavilion Gardens. This rather oriental-looking building was designed by William ?dford Bryden and opened in June 1899. It was later used as a promenade bandstand and the orchestra played there on ?e afternoons in the 1930s. Built almost entirely of wood and glass, the building was allowed to deteriorate and was used ? the 1960s as an amusement arcade. It was demolished due to its unsafe condition in the 1970s.

?6.   Solomon's Temple, or Grin Low Tower, designed by G. E. Garlick was built by public subscription and officially ?ened by Mr. Victor Cavendish M.P. in September 1896. It replaced a tower reputedly built to provide work for the ? employed of Buxton in about 1835. It stands at an altitude of 1,440 ft. on a Bronze Age barrow which was excavated ? local archaeologist, Micah Salt, during 1894. In recent times the tower has been repaired and continues to provide a ?al landmark.

127. Corbar Wood and walks. As with Grin Woods and Solomon's Temple to the south, Corbar Wood was, and still is, a popular area for walking, although little remains of the paths shown in this view. The steep ascent through the woods and to the top of Corbar Hill is rewarded by fine views of the town to the south and the moorlands to the north, leading to Lightwood Reservoir. The gritstone outcrops on Corbar differ sharply from the limestone predominant to the south of the town.

128. Sylvan Park was one of two public recreation grounds available to Buxtonians before the turn of the century. The park had a bandstand which stood on land to the right of the picture. It is thought that the Romans built a road through Sylvan Park, descending from their settlement on Silverlands and thence through Fairfield and via Batham Gate to Brough.

29.   Coach trips were a very popular Victorian pastime and visits were made to Chatsworth, Axe Edge, Millers Dale and other Peak District beauty spots. The Hot Baths end of the Crescent was a regular departure point and this view dates to 1910.

130. A trip to the *Cat and Fiddle Inn* between Buxton and Macclesfield, about five miles from Buxton, proved an interesting drive for the visitor. Situated at an altitude of 1,690 ft., it is the second highest inn in England and offers the tourist unsurpassed views. This illustration shows the thriving carriage trade in operation.

131. Ice-skating on the frozen lake in the Pavilion Gardens. Precautions were taken against drowning accidents by lowering the level of the lake before it was frozen.

132. From 1884 the Buxton Improvements Company ran an Open Lawn Tennis tournament which continued until 1954. The competition included the Derbyshire Ladies' and Gentlemen's Singles and the All-England Ladies' Doubles, the latter national championship also being staged at Buxton until 1954. Tennis was also a popular sport for visitors and residents.

133.   The Pavilion Gardens curling rink was opened in 1906. The rink, or more precisely, three rinks, was a shallow pond which could be used for both curling and ice-skating when it was frozen over during the winter months. The Buxton Curling Club was founded in 1895 by Dr. Graeme Dickson, proprietor of Wye House, a private asylum.

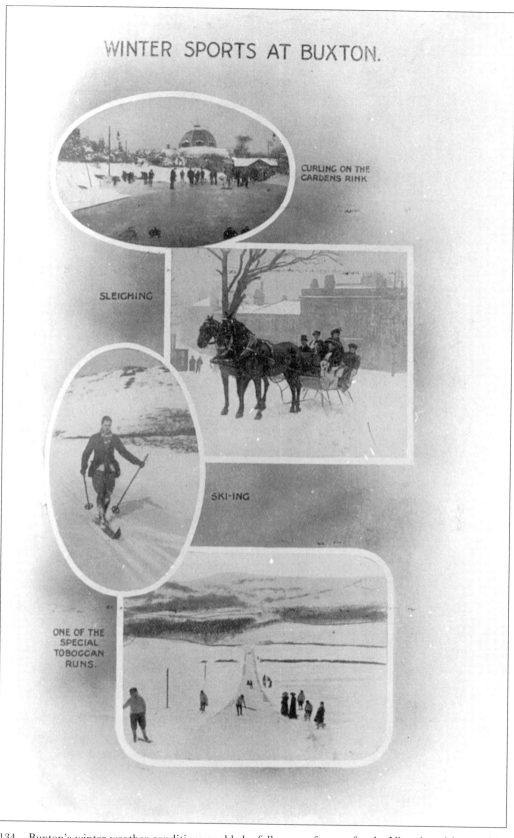

WINTER SPORTS AT BUXTON.

CURLING ON THE GARDENS RINK

SLEIGHING

SKI-ING

ONE OF THE SPECIAL TOBOGGAN RUNS.

134.   Buxton's winter weather conditions enabled a full range of sports for the Victorian visitor as this illustration shows. In particular it was possible to ski, sleigh and toboggan on the snow-packed roads, an option which is, unfortunately, no longer available today.

135.   External view of the Hot Baths just after the re-modelling of 1900 when the original glass and iron colonnading of 1854 was removed. This 'classical' stone frontage was soon embellished with glass once again as later illustrations show. However, the Hot Baths building today looks much like this photograph.

136.   This view of c.1905 shows the bathchairmen waiting for business opposite the Hot Baths. Patients would be wheeled around the town to the different baths for treatment and to the various beauty spots around Buxton. In addition to the Hot Baths there were bathchair stands at both ends of Broadwalk. The bathchairs were so designed that the passenger could be completely enclosed and protected from the elements to and from a visit to the baths. The business of the bathchairmen dwindled and eventually finished at about the start of the Second World War.

7. In 1901 a variety of treatments was offered using the
celebrated natural mineral water at both the Hot and Natural
Baths. These were priced individually and included: private bath
1s. 6d., needle bath 2s. 6d., vapour bath with immersion bath and
shower 3s. 6d. Entry was by ticket only.

A FEW OF THE 87 TREATMENTS ADMINISTERED AT
BUXTON BATHS

THE BUXTON
DOUCHE
MASSAGE

ONE OF THE
PRIVATE
IMMERSION BATHS

A CORNER OF THE
LADIES' SWIMMING
POOL

ONE OF THE
ROOMS IN THE
ELECTRICAL
DEPARTMENT

38. The gentlemen's bath in the natural wing was sited directly
over the main thermal spring. The water passed upwards into the
bath through holes in the marble floor and the excess water
overflowed into the other baths in the building. This spring is now
covered by a perspex dome and is used to supply the Buxton
Mineral Water Company. The hospital baths and the public
swimming bath are also supplied with natural mineral water. It is
on or near this site that a Roman bath has been discovered. An
excavation of the main spring in 1974/75 uncovered a votive
offering of many Roman coins.

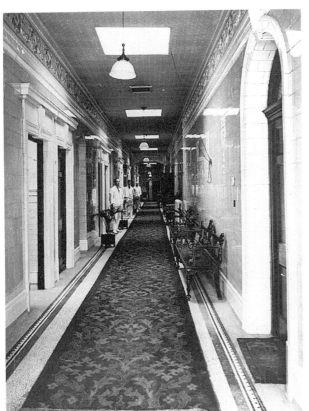

139. A view of the gentlemen's corridor of the Hot Baths. Both sexes entered by the same entrance at the south frontage but used separate corridors to the treatment rooms. The baths building is now a shopping arcade but before the building was converted for this purpose, the authors remember seeing a full length mirror at the end of the ladies' corridor with a printed warning above it asking the ladies to make sure that they were properly dressed before they met up with the gentlemen round the corner!

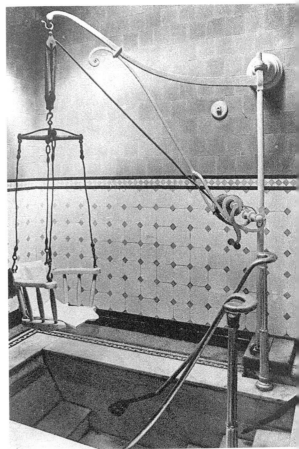

140. Small plunge bath at the Hot Baths with a pulley chair arrangement which enabled invalid patients to be lowered easily into the water. An example of one of these baths has been preserved in the Cavendish Arcade.

41.   In 1909 new colonnading was built on to the front of the Hot Baths, re-using some of the old and introducing coloured glass together with facilities for electric lighting. It was designed by local architects Bryden and Walton. The glass colonnading was removed in the early 1970s due to its unsafe condition.

142.   In addition to the baths built around the Crescent there was a further private bath known as the Tonic Bath which was built in 1793 by Dr. Norton on the site of a cold spring. The water was heated by flues beneath the bath. This early aerial view of the junction of West Road, Macclesfield Road and Burlington Road shows a semi-cylindrical structure to the left of centre which is the roof covering the Tonic Bath (circled). It was more recently used as a public swimming bath but nowadays nothing remains of it and the site is built upon.

143.   Buxton Opera House was opened in 1903 and designed by the famous theatre architect, Frank Matcham. The theatre was used as a cinema from 1932 but gradually fell into disrepair. It was completely refurbished and reopened in 1979 with the first Buxton International Opera Festival, which is now an annual event. The theatre has a truly magnificent interior and attracts audiences from great distances with a wide and varied programme of entertainments.

144. Opera House programme of 1909.

145. Buxton baths are renowned for visits of royalty. Perhaps the most famous was Mary, Queen of Scots who came to take the waters on several occasions between 1573-84. In the 19th century Princess Victoria stayed at the *Great Hotel* in 1832 and returned as Queen Victoria in Ma[y] 1899. In January 1905 King Edward VII and Queen Alexandra visited the baths, the Devonshire Hospital and t[he] Pavilion Gardens during their tour of the town.

6.   The *Empire Hotel* was built by Spiers and Pond between 1901-3 at a cost of £150,000. Although an imposing building, s existence as a hotel was brief and it ceased trading in 1914. During the First World War it was used as an annexe to e Granville Military Hospital and as a discharge depot for Canadian troops after the war. It was demolished in 1964 but is particular photograph shows the gateposts which still remain on Carlisle Road.

147.   Eagle Parade, 1900. At the turn of the century Higher Buxton was also being developed and this fine row of houses and shops was built by local architect, G. E. Garlick. Comparison should be made with Plate 43 which shows the same area in the 1870s. To make way for this building the old Buxton College, the shops of Hargreaves, the china merchants and Rowlands butchers had to be demolished. The market cross is shown here in its earlier position at the north end of the market-place.

8. Spring Gardens looking east, *c*.1907. Formerly known 'Town Street' or 'Bakewell Road', it became a busy nmercial street in Victorian times. Many of the shops were nted with cast-iron and glass colonnading. The *Royal Hotel* y be seen on the left and further down on the right was the *kespeare Hotel*. R. R. Duke, the builder and architect, had offices at 31 Spring Gardens.

149. Spring Gardens, *c*.1907, looking west from Sylvan Park. Several of the Victorian buildings on the right remain today. At this end of Spring Gardens a small fountain was erected in 1886. It was donated by the local solicitor, J. W. Taylor, and is made from granite to a design supplied by the Metropolitan Drinking Fountain Association. It is usually dressed by children for the annual well-dressing festival.

0. In Scarsdale Place, Higher Buxton was the business of Holme and Ash, probably the best known ironmongery shop the town. Scarsdale Place was named to commemorate Lord Scarsdale who owned this land. The photograph shows the mmonplace practice of displaying wares on the street outside.

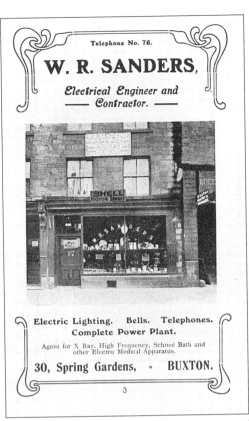

151.   Advertisement for W. R. Sanders, Electrical Engineer and Contractor, whose business was in Spring Gardens. Electricity was introduced to Buxton in 1900, followed shortly by the telephone. Sanders would have supplied electrical equipment to the Buxton baths and hydros which were amongst the first of the public buildings to be lit by electricity. The business later went on to become Sanders Garage which was acquired by the Kenning Motor Company.

152.   Shufflebotham's ironmonger's shop, 56 Spring Gardens, c.1907. The proprietor, John Edward Shufflebotham, is seen in the doorway. As well as being an ironmonger and cycle salesman, he was also a pioneer motorcyclist. The shop is presently occupied by A. T. Mays, travel agents.

3. The *Shakespeare Hotel*, *c*.1908. Built in 1711, the name of the hotel probably derives from the old theatre which stood nearby in Spring Gardens. The hotel changed hands and was altered many times before it was demolished and replaced by the Woolworths Emporium in 1926.

Shakespeare Hotel Family and Commercial

Established 1711. Entirely Renovated.
Largest **GARAGE & STABLING IN BUXTON.**
Inspection Pit. New Lounge.
Large and light Stock Rooms. Excellent Cuisine.
Large Stock of carefully-selected Spirits, Wines & Cigars.
Billiards. Telephone 480.
Telegrams : "Shakespeare, Buxton." E. Köhli, **Manager**

4. Advertisement for the *Shakespeare Hotel*. The open archway in the centre of the building is the only remaining part of the original hotel. The name of the hotel's manager, E. Kohli, reflects the continental influence which was prevalent in the hotel trade at that time. The motor repair garage which today is situated behind the Woolworth shop was until recently still known as the Shakespeare Garage.

Royal Hotel,
BUXTON.

TELEGRAMS:
"ROYAL" BUXTON.
TELEPHONE 0495.

SPECIAL WEEK-END
TERMS.

THE LOUNGE.

American Elevator. Electric Light throughout. 50 Bedrooms.
Spacious Public and Private Rooms.
Level with Baths. Near Pavilion Gardens and Golf Links (18 Holes).
Private Grounds.
Table d'Hôte. Separate Tables. Excellent Cuisine.
Illustrated Tariff on application.

Headquarters of the Publishers' Representatives during Conference
Week, 1903.

C. TESSIER DUNHAM, Manager (late West Cliff Hotel, Folkestone).

155. The interior of the *Royal Hotel* in 1903 showing the newly-installed electric lighting. The hotel had undergone extensive enlargement and alteration in 1882 to the designs of R. R. Duke, whose job it had been to superintend the erection of the hotel some thirty years earlier. The hotel had an octagonal billiard room built on to the rear of the building and this rather unusual looking extension was demolished when the Spring Gardens Shopping Centre was built.

156. The *Crescent Hotel* was run by the Smilter family for many years during the last century. Not surprisingly, they used this photograph of the magnificent hotel dining room in their advertising. It was originally the assembly and ballroom of the *Crescent* designed by Carr and opened in 1784. It has an ornate Adam style ceiling plastered by James Henderson of York. In more recent times it has housed the reference section of the Public Library.

157.   In addition to the spa trade, a major source of employment for Buxton people in the 19th century was quarry work in the many limestone quarries which encircled the town. Fierce commercial competition existed between quarry owners, but in 1891 more than twelve firms merged to form the Buxton Lime Firms Co. Ltd. This photograph shows Buxton Central Quarry viewed from Topley Pike on the Bakewell road out of the town.

158.   A quarry face after the main blasting had taken place showing the use of 'new technology' in 1908. A compressed air drill is being used to prepare a large lump of stone for further blasting, in order to break it down in size. This process was known as 'popping' and, prior to the introduction of compressed air, the stone would be drilled by hand using a long bar.

159. Limestone was burned in kilns to produce lime or quicklime. This had an increasing number of uses in the new industrial methods being discovered, for example, in textile and chemical manufacture and in the building industry. Shown here is the lime kiln and portion of the quarry at the Dowlow Lime & Stone Co. works in 1908.

160. Though much used as a building material, quarried limestone was also used for garden decoration. The limestone was 'weathered' for some time in an exposed position until natural erosion smoothed the rough edges of the stones giving them a more rounded or sculptured appearance. Examples of such stones can still be seen in many of the town's private and public gardens.

61. A view of the *Grove Hotel*, *c*.1910, showing the glass-roofed colonnade which extended around the corner and down Spring Gardens. The Midland Railway station building can be seen on the left. The occasion is a well-dressing and Turner's memorial, decorated with flowers, can just be seen to the left of the picture.

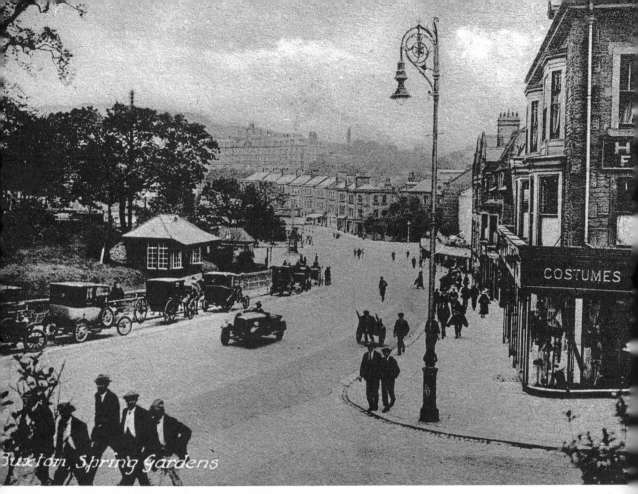

Buxton, Spring Gardens

162. An incorrectly titled photograph, this is actually Terrace Road leading from Lower to Higher Buxton. On the right is London House, the draper's shop belonging to J. W. Potter which was established by 1872 and still remains today. The hut-like building at the left of the road was the taxi rank.

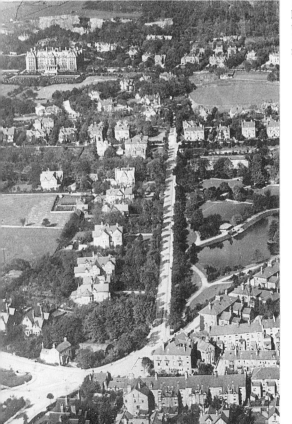

163. To complete this history are two aerial views offering a wide panorama of the town taken in the early years of the 20th century. Th shows the full length of Burlington Road. The *Empire Hotel* is seen at top left and the cricket field top right. Lismore fields can be seen in th left middle area. These fields had been unploughed through the ag and a recent archaeological excavation has revealed evidence of Mesolithic and Neolithic occupation. The fields have recently bee built upon.

54. The second aerial view captures many of the important features of the town. The two railway stations on the top right
re balanced by the *Palace Hotel* on the left. The Georgian Crescent is the centrepiece but the Devonshire Royal Hospital
ome and complex offers fine architectural support. On the bottom right can be seen the Town Hall still with its open
rcades. To the left are the Pavilion Gardens and opposite are the Slopes (with very few trees at this time).

165. And finally, two crests used in Buxton during the period of our history and both designed by R. R. Duke. A common seal originally designed for the *Palace Hotel* in 1868 and subsequently used by the Freemasons, the football clubs, Buxton College and the Local Board. The coat of arms, was presented by him to the town at the opening of the Pump Room in 1894

Practical Cameras,

With McKellen's Patent Spiral Screw Changing System, absolutely reliable.

Fig. P151.

A High-class Automatic Magazine Hand Camera.

The special feature of this Camera is the **changing system**, which is of the **simplest possible description**. In the words of a distinguished amateur, "The extraordinary thing about it is that no one has ever thought of it before." It consists of a screw running across the top of and at right angles to the sheaths. The sheaths rest on guide rails, and the rounded edge of each sheath takes into one of the grooves of the screw, the front sheath in the front groove, and so on. The screw is attached to a handle which projects through the back and lies flat. In its normal position it fits on a pin or stud which prevents it from being accidentally moved; at the front end a guide pin projects in the same direction as the handle.

SPECIFICATION.

Measurement—8¼ × 6 × 5 inches.　　**Size**—Quarter-plate (4¼ × 3¼).
Capacity—12 Plates or Films in sheaths.
Changing Arrangement—McKellen's Patent Spiral Screw, **absolutely reliable**.
Finders—Two Ground Glass, giving correct images.
Shutter—Everset, with Iris Diaphragm, giving "Time," "Prolonged," or "Instantaneous" exposures.
Covering—(No. 8) Cloth, (Nos. 10 and 12) **Finest Morocco** Leather.
Lens—(Nos. 8 and 10) Achromatic Landscape of excellent quality, (No. 12) **Rapid Rectilinear**, working at ƒ8.
Counter—Automatic.

PRICES.

No. 8 CAMERA, as Specification, with Achromatic Lens, and covered in Cloth　　£1　1　0

No. 10 CAMERA, as Specification, with Achromatic Lens, and covered in Morocco Leather　　£1　5　0

No. 12 CAMERA, as Specification, with Superior Rapid Rectilinear Lens, working at ƒ8, and Improved Shutter, and covered in Morocco Leather　　£2　10　0

PHOTOGRAPHS OF THE NEW GARDENS, BUXTON

PUBLISHED BY
B. W. BENTLEY,

Of The QUADRANT, BUXTON.　　Branch Establishments—St. Ann's-square, Manchester, And EAGLE PARADE, Buxton.

(From *The Reliquary*, April, 1875.)

PORTRAITS OF THE CAVENDISH FAMILY.—Mr. B. W. Bentley, of Buxton and Manchester, to whose admirable series of photographic views of Buxton and its gardens we have already directed attention, has just prepared a series of portraits of the members of the family to whom, more than any other, this country is indebted for many of the blessings and advantages which it enjoys. We allude, of course, to the family of Cavendish, with which Derbyshire is so intimately and happily connected, and to whom its inhabitants owe such constant, such liberal, and such open-handed and generous help over every project for its or their good. First and foremost among these portraits must be named those of His Grace the Duke of Devonshire (both cabinet size and carte-de-visite), Lord Lieutenant of the county, Chancellor of the University of Cambridge, and one of the most enlightened and liberal-minded of the English aristocracy. This portrait will be, indeed, a boon to all who have the happiness to know His Grace. It is not only a "speaking likeness," but is *life itself*; and, being the latest taken of him, shows him *as he is*, and with that happy, quiet, benevolent look on his face which is so well remembered by those who have had the happiness to come in contact with him. It is a great success, and is, indeed, a marvel of photographic art. Next we have a life-like portrait of the Duke's brother, our excellent and valued representative, Lord George H. Cavendish, M.P. for North Derbyshire. Of this portrait it is enough to say it is of cabinet size, and arranged in every way as a companion to the Duke's picture. So deservedly popular—nay, so much beloved—is Lord George throughout the division, that we opine there is not one of his political, as well as personal friends but will feel gratified at being able, through the exercise of Mr. Bentley's skill, to secure and possess so excellent a likeness. Lord George has represented Derbyshire in Parliament for an unbroken period of more than forty years; and we earnestly hope he may be spared in health and strength many, many years yet to come, to continue to represent it. Should he ever cease to do so, we trust it will only be to be transferred to the Upper House, as a peer in his own right, a recognition of his valuable services to which he is more than entitled. Next, are excellent portraits of Lady Louisa Cavendish, wife of Lord George, and of their son, Colonel Cavendish. They are striking and excellent likenesses, those of Lady George being peculiarly successful and happy achievements of art. Another portrait represents in all the goodness and simplicity of his character, the late Lord Richard Cavendish, brother to the Duke, and another is a speaking likeness of Lord Edward Cavendish, the Duke's third son. Mr. Bentley has long been known as one of the most successful and clever of artists, whether in the field of landscape or that of portraiture, and the present series give him a rank above many of his contemporaries. He studies the *pose* of the figures with an artist's eye, and his manipulation is that of an accomplished operator. We accord high praise to these evidences of his taste and skill.

(From *The Art Journal*, July, 1872.)

There are few—if there be any—places in the kingdom so attractive as Buxton: first, it is proverbially health-giving; from the days of the Romans to our own, its baths and waters have been famous for cures of many ailments—rheumatism more especially; their power has not been weakened by time; there are thousands of rich and poor who owe a deep debt of gratitude to the balmy airs and refreshing waters of this long-favoured resort of the ailing. It is cheerful without being gay; there are always amusements enough, yet regular hours and temperate habits are essential aids to cures. Moreover, it is in the heart of picturesque Derbyshire; a hundred sources of pleasure, from landscape beauties, wild and grand, or richly cultivated, are within easy reach; the best of the dales are at "driving distances," some may be visited by easy walks; the "Duke's Drive," that skirts the town, is unsurpassed for a rare combination of wild magnificence with tree-clad beauties. Add to these attractions that princely Chatsworth and romantic Haddon are less than a score of miles off, and that public and private conveyances conduct daily to these delights of the tourist. Buxton is not only a lure to the invalid, the convalescent can visit no place in England that presents so many temptations.

But the venerable, interesting, and picturesque town itself has abundant charms, as all will admit who examine these admirable photographs; its terrace, gardens, promenades, bridges, cascades, fern-clad rocks, and umbrageous walks, lined with "Patrician trees and Plebeian underwood." They seem like creations of fancy, instead of copies of actual facts, and cannot fail to tempt many who see them to make their summer or autumn holidays in this long renowned and most charming "watering-place." Mr. Bentley has certainly conferred an obligation on the town; and we hope its authorities have appreciated his merits and recompensed him according to his deserts. As mere photographs they rank with the very best that have been produced anywhere by any artist; both skill and knowledge have been manifested in the selection of subjects. A more attractive series of views does not exist; it is difficult to understand that they are all of "bits" in the town, or immediately adjacent to it.
